Mandarin Chinese
in 30 Days

By De-an Wu Swihart

Course Book

Berlitz Publishing
New York   Munich   Singapore

Contacting the Editors
Every effort has been made to provide accurate information in this publication, but changes are inevitable. The publisher cannot be responsible for any resulting loss, inconvenience or injury. We would appreciate it if readers would call our attention to any errors or outdated information by contacting Berlitz Publishing, 193 Morris Avenue, Springfield, NJ 07081, USA. Fax: 1-908-206-1103. email: comments@berlitzbooks.com

Berlitz Trademark Reg. U.S. Patent Office and other countries. Marca Registrada. Used under license from Berlitz Investment Corporation

Publishing Director: Sheryl Olinsky Borg
Editor/Project Manager: Emily Bernath
Senior Editor: Lorraine Sova
Editor: Monica Bentley
Cover design: Claudia Petrilli

Cover photo © DIOMEDIA/Alamy

Printed in China, May 2007

Contents

Introduction

Mandarin Chinese in 30 Days is a self-study course that, in a short time, will provide you with a sound basic knowledge of Mandarin Chinese. This book is designed to teach Chinese step by step, in a logical progression. The language and subjects in this book provide context-based, authentic situations to help you learn what you really need to know and progress more quickly in your learning. In 30 lessons you will acquire both an active and a passive understanding of the language, enabling you to function effectively in day-to-day life in China.

The audio CDs contain vocabulary, dialogues and exercises. When you see 🔊 in the book, that tells you that you should listen to the CD to hear words pronounced, listen to a dialogue or practice with an interactive listening comprehension exercise. Each lesson has its own track, so you can easily find your place on the CD and move back to earlier lessons to review.

The 30 lessons are presented in groups of three under 10 topics, each providing language relevant to daily life. The lessons are numbered 1-30, but are also identified as Part A, Part B and Part C so that you can easily recognize which aspect of the topic you are studying.

Part A

The first lesson of each topic, also called Part A, will teach you the vocabulary you need to communicate on that subject. All of the words in the vocabulary list are recorded on the audio, so you can listen as you learn, and practice with the audio later. The vocabulary lessons end with one or two short dialogues. The dialogues will show you the vocabulary in context, and will also preview the grammar that you will learn in the next lesson.

Part B

The next lesson, Part B, will focus on grammar. Before you start the new material of the lesson, you should take a few minutes to review the vocabulary you learned in Part A, and to read the dialogue(s) again. This quick review will help you learn more effectively, and better remember what you've learned.

In Part B, you will learn important points about grammar, sentence structure and pronunciation. The points that you learn are linked to the dialogues so that you can see and hear the grammar in context. Grammar practice sections also give you the opportunity to use the new grammar in context, and review the rules you've learned.

Part C

The third lesson of each topic, Part C, contains review exercises and information about Chinese customs and culture. Before you begin Part C, be sure to review both the vocabulary and the grammar that you learned in the previous two lessons. Re-read the dialogue(s), listening to the CD to practice your pronunciation, and make sure that you understand the grammar points. Then, move on to the writing and listening exercises in Part C.

Once you finish the exercises in Part C and check your answers, you have completed that topic. The next chapter will begin a new topic, and will again be subtitled "Part A" to indicate that it includes new vocabulary and dialogues.

Mandarin Chinese

Many television programs in China are captioned with Chinese characters. Why? China has many regional dialects, and their pronunciation can differ as much as Italian does from Portuguese, although the written characters are the same throughout China and wherever Chinese is spoken. For many centuries, in imperial China, Mandarin was the official dialect (**Guānhuà** 官话), and was spoken by officials throughout China. Then in 1919 the government designated Mandarin as the "National Language" (**Guóyǔ** 国语), using the Beijing dialect as the standard for pronunciation and the vernacular Northern dialect as the standard for vocabulary and grammar. Since the establishment of the People's Republic of China in 1949, Mandarin has been referred to as "Common Speech" (**Pǔtōnghuà** 普通话); Taiwan has continued to use the name "**Guóyǔ**." Today, Mandarin is the standard Chinese speech and the official medium of communication throughout China, and is also the local spoken language in fourteen provinces and for 73 percent of the population of China. The language you will be learning in this book is Mandarin.

There are seven other major dialects of Chinese, each of which is native to one or two provinces in southeastern China.

Besides Mandarin, the other major dialects of Chinese are:

The Northern Dialect

The Northern dialect (Běifāng fāngyán 北方方言) (spoken by 73 percent of Chinese people) is spoken in many provinces, including Héběi, Hénán, Shāndōng, Shānxī, Shǎnxī, Yúnnán, Guìzhōu, Sìchuān, Ānhuī, Húběi, and northern Jiāngsū.

The Wú Dialect

The Wú 吴 dialect (spoken by 8 percent of Chinese people) is spoken in the area around Jiāngsū and Shànghǎi. Wú is the old name of Jiāngsū province.

The Xiāng Dialect

The Xiāng 湘 dialect (spoken by 5 percent of Chinese people) is spoken in and around Húnán province. Xiāng is the old name of Húnán province.

The Yuè Dialect

The Yuè 粤 dialect, or Cantonese (Guǎngdōnghuà 广东话), (spoken by 5 percent of Chinese people) is spoken in Guǎngdōng, Hong Kong, Macao, Singapore, and by many overseas Chinese around the world.

The Hakka Dialect

The Hakka dialect (Kèjiāhuà 客家话) (spoken by 4.3 percent of Chinese people) is spoken in Guǎngxī, Fújiàn, Singapore, and Taiwan.

The Gàn Dialect

The Gàn 赣 dialect (Jiāngxīhuà 江西话) (spoken by 1.7 percent of Chinese people) is spoken in and around Jiāngxī. Gàn is the old name of Jiāngxī province.

The Mǐn Dialect

The Mǐn 闽 dialect is divided into Southern Mǐn and Northern Mǐn dialects. Two percent of Chinese people speak Southern Mǐn; they are in the southern part of Fújiàn province, which is centered around the capital city of Xiàmén, and in Taiwan and Singapore. It is called "Mǐnnánhuà 闽南话" or "Xiàménhuà 厦门话." One percent of Chinese people speak Northern Min; they are in the northern part of Fújiàn, around Fúzhōu.

Pinyin: Part A

The Pinyin System

Pinyin is a romanized phonetic writing system for Chinese based on the national standard system of pronunciation. It was officially adopted by the Chinese government in 1958 in order to help speakers of other dialects learn the standard pronunciation. It has also become the main system of romanization outside of China. Today it is widely used on street signs, store signs, and in book titles, as well as in books, magazines and newspapers for non-native speakers of Chinese. Pinyin is also used to input characters in Chinese computer word-processing systems. Pinyin can help English speakers accurately pronounce any Chinese character.

A Pinyin syllable has three components: an initial, a final, and a tone mark that indicates the pitch contour. There are twenty-one initials, thirty-eight finals, and four tones.

Pinyin uses all of the English letters (except "v") to form a phonetic alphabet. In this book, we will use English as a point of reference for learning Pinyin, but keep in mind that many Pinyin sounds are slightly different from English or have no equivalents in English because Pinyin was not designed just for speakers of English.

Initials

Initials are similar to consonants in English, but English consonants can appear anywhere in a word, not just at the beginning. Initials are always placed at the beginning of a syllable. They can be divided into six groups based on their phonetic characteristics.

▶

b, p, m, f (Labials)

Formed using the lips. Pronounced the same as in English.

b-   p-   m-   f-

d, t, n, l (Dentals)

Formed with the tongue touching or near the back of the upper teeth. Pronounced the same as in English.

d-   t-   n-   l-

g, k, h (Velars)

Formed from the throat. "G" and "k" are the same as in English, but "h" is slightly more guttural or aspirated than the English "h" and more like the German "ch" in "ach."

g-   k-   h-

The pronunciation of the next three groups usually requires extra attention by English speakers.

j, q, x (Frontals)

Formed with the tip of the tongue directly against the back of the lower teeth. Unlike English, the tip of the tongue does not touch the roof of the mouth. The tongue curves, with its upper front surface touching just behind the ridge behind the upper teeth. The lips must be tight and pulled widely apart, as in a forced smile.

Frontal	Pronunciation	Example
j-	ji, jee, gee	Jimmy, jeep
q-	chee	cheese, chip
x-	shee	ship, sheer

z, c, s (Aveolars)

Formed with the tip of the tongue touching or near the base of the lower teeth and with the upper teeth in contact with the upper front surface of the tongue. Be alert to avoid the tendency of some English speakers to pronounce "c" incorrectly as "k" (instead of as "ts").

Aveolar	Pronunciation	Example
z-	z, dz, ds	kids, woods
c-	ts	its, cats, rats
s-	(same as English)	sense, step

zh, ch, sh, r (Retroflexes)

Formed with the tip of the tongue rolled upward and touching the roof of the mouth. When you say "r" in Chinese the lips should be less open than in English. You will feel the air vibrating around your tongue. Your lower jaw is thrust slightly forward.

Retroflex	Pronunciation	Example
zh-	dj	bridge
ch-	ch	chat
sh-	sh	shore
r-	cross between "j" and "r"	no English equivalent

Finals

Finals are composed of up to four letters. All thirty-eight finals are made from six single vowels (a, e, i, o, u, ü), which can be combined with three consonant endings (n, ng, r). All the finals are listed in this chart. Many vowel sounds in Chinese do not have English equivalents, so pay attention to the pronunciation on the CD.

Final	By itself	Pronunciation	Examples
-a	**a**	ah	ah, father
-ai	**ai**	i	rise, my, eye
-an	**an**	ahn	analyze
-ang	**ang**	ahng	gong
-ao	**ao**	ow	how
-e	**e**	uh	(no English equivalent)
-ei		ay	eight, pay
-en	**en**	un	run
-eng		ung	pungent
-er		ur	car, curve (cross between "ar" and "er")
-o		similar to Chinese "uo" (begin with lips puckered; end with lips apart)	wore, woman
-ong	**awng**	(like "wrong" but with rounder "o" sound)	Hong Kong
-ou	**ou**	oh (begin with lips apart; end with lips puckered)	go, owe

Spelling Changes

When i, u, ü Are Semi-Vowels

When the finals i, u, ü (and any compound using i, u, ü, such as ia, uang, üan) are not preceded by an initial, they are called semi-vowels, which means they actually function as initials. In these cases, their spelling changes as shown:

   change "i" to "y" when "i" is at the initial position

   change "u" to "w" when "w" is at the initial positioin

   change "ü" to "yu" when "ü" is at the initial position

   change "i" to "yi" when "i" is by itself

   change "u" to "wu" when "u" is by itself

Final	Spelling change	English sound
-i	yi	ee
-ia	ya	ee-ah (said as one syllable)
-ian	yan	ee-en (said as one syllable)
-iang	yang	ee-ahng
-iao	yao	ee-ow (said as one syllable)
-ie	ye	ee-eh (said as one syllable), "i" is shorter and softer than "e"
-in	yin	een
-ing	ying	ing
-iong	yong	ee-ong (said as one syllable)
-iu	yu	e-o (said as one syllable)
-u	wu	oo
-ua	wa	wah
-uai	wai	wai
-uan	wan	wahn
-uang	wang	wahng

-ueng	weng	oo-ung
-ui	wei	way
-un	wen	wun
-uo	wo	no English equivalent, similar to Chinese "-o"; wore (begin with lips puckered out; end with lips apart); woman
-ü	yu	like French "eu" or German "ü"; no English equivalent; used only after "n" or "I"
-üan	yuan	"y" as in Yvonne plus "e"; no English equivalent
-üe	yue	weh, oo-eh (said like one syllable); "y" as in Yvonne plus "an"; no English equivalent
-ün	yun	"y" as in Yvonne plus "n"; no English equivalent

Spelling Changes of the Final ü

When ü follows j-, q-, or x- in a syllable, it changes to u, as in these examples:

jü → juan	jue	jun
qü → quan	que	qun
xü → xuan	xue	xun

Tones

Each syllable in Chinese has a tone. In spoken Chinese, changing the tone of a syllable changes its meaning. For instance, "qu" in the 3rd tone means "a man marries a woman", but "qu" in the 4th tone means "to go."

The diagrams below illustrate each of the four tones:

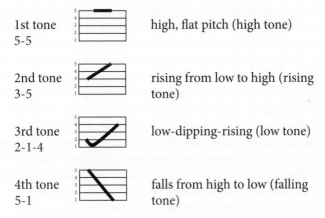

1st tone
5-5   high, flat pitch (high tone)

2nd tone
3-5   rising from low to high (rising tone)

3rd tone
2-1-4   low-dipping-rising (low tone)

4th tone
5-1   falls from high to low (falling tone)

In the Pinyin system, the tone mark is placed above the vowel. If there are two vowels in a final, the tone mark is placed above the first vowel, except that when the first vowel is "i", "u", or "ü," the tone mark is placed above the second vowel. Examples: liù, duì, yuán. Chinese characters are not written with tone marks.

On the CD you can hear the four different tones of "ma."

mā	má	mǎ	mà
妈 *mother*	麻 *hemp*	马 *horse*	骂 *curse*

Neutral Tone

Chinese also has a neutral tone, which has no tone mark and is unstressed. A neutral tone always follows a major-toned syllable and never comes at the beginning of a phrase:

tāde   his   (1st tone followed by a neutral tone)
tāmende theirs (1st tone followed by two neutral tones)

A neutral tone is shorter and lighter than major-toned syllables. However there are two levels of pitch for neutral tones, depending on the tone of the previous syllable:

Low neutral tone

When a neutral tone follows a 1st, 2nd, or 4th tone, it is pronounced in a lower pitch:

gēge   elder brother
yéye   grandfather

High neutral tone

When a neutral tone follows a 3rd tone, it is pronounced in a higher pitch:

jiějie   elder sister
wǎnshang evening

Tone Changes

Yī (one), **qī** (seven), **bā** (eight), **bù** (no) can have several different tones. Keep in mind that:

1. **Yī** can have three different tones: 1st (when used alone), 2nd (when before a 4th tone) or 4th (when before a 1st, 2nd or 3rd tone)

2. **Qī** and **bā** each can have two tones: 1st tone or 2nd tone (when followed by a 4th tone).

3. 不 **bù** (no) can be 4th tone or 2nd tone (when followed by a 4th tone).

3+3 → 2+3

If a 3rd tone is followed by another 3rd tone, the first 3rd tone is pronounced as a 2nd tone although the printed tone mark does not change:

nǐ hǎo → **ní hǎo**   Hello! How do you do!
hěn měi → **hén měi**   very beautiful

Half-3rd Tone

When a 3rd tone is followed by a 1st, 2nd, or 4th tone, the 3rd tone is pronounced as a half-3rd tone (which only falls but does not rise), although the printed tone mark does not change:

měitiān   every day
Měiguó   America
mǎipiào   buy a ticket

Syllable Division Marks

When a syllable beginning with "a," "o," or "e" follows another syllable and could cause confusion about how the syllables should be divided, an apostrophe (') is added in front of the second syllable.

For example: **Xī'ān** (西安 a city name)
might be confused with: **xiān** (先 first).

Each of the three components of a Chinese syllable—initial, final, and tone—is important. Incorrect pronunciation of any component can result in misunderstanding. Pay careful attention to each syllable's tone and practice the tones now, at the very beginning of your study of Chinese. Doing so will give you a solid foundation for effective communication in Chinese.

Pinyin: Part B

Pronunciation Practice

🔘 Read the following aloud, being careful to pronounce the tones correctly. Refer to the CD to check your pronunciation.

a. The four tones of yi, in order and in reverse order:

| yī | yí | yǐ | yì | | yì | yǐ | yí | yī |

b. The four tones of er:

| ér | ěr | (ēr) | èr | | ěr | èr | ér | (ēr) |

c. sān vs. sǎn:

| sān | sǎn | sǎn | sān | | sǎn | sān | sān | sǎn |

d. sī vs. sì:

| sī | sì | sì | sī | | sì | sī | sī | sì |

e. wǔ vs. wù

| wǔ | wù | wǔ | wù | | wù | wǔ | wù | wǔ |

f. liù vs. liú:

| liù | liú | liù | liú | | liú | liù | liú | liù |

g. qī vs. qǐ

| qī | qǐ | qǐ | qī | | qǐ | qī | qī | qǐ |

🔘 Read aloud these common Chinese surnames. Refer
to the CD to check your pronunciation. You'll also hear
the numbers read in Chinese before each name. You'll
learn these in depth later.

1) Chén	7) Jiǎ	13) Liú	19) Xiè
2) Dèng	8) Jīn	14) Mèng	20) Yáng
3) Féng	9) Kǒng	15) Shěn	21) Zhāng
4) Gāo	10) Lǐ	16) Sūn	22) Zhào
5) Guō	11) Liáng	17) Tián	23) Zhèng
6) Huáng	12) Lín	18) Wú	24) Zhōu

🔘 Read the following words aloud, paying special
attention to the tones. Refer to the CD to check your
pronunciation.

1+1:

fēijī (airplane)   shāfā (sofa)   shūbāo (school
bag)   Xiāngshān (Fragrant Hills)   huāshēng (peanut)

1+1+1:

Zhījiāgē (Chicago)

2+2:

Chángchéng (Great Wall)   shítáng (cafeteria)   yínháng
(bank)   yóutiáo (fried bread)   Huánghé (Yellow River)

2+2+2

Yíhéyuán (Summer Palace)

4+4:

fàndiàn (hotel)   sùshè (dormitory)   diànhuà
(telephone)   bàogào (report)   zàijiàn (good-bye)

4+4+4:

diànshìjù (soap opera)

🔘 Each entry below has an initial sound and a final sound that combine to form complete words. Read the initial and final sounds separately, then read the full word. Check your pronunciation on the audio.

Group A	Group B	Group C
w -àn	zh -āng	ch -én
j -iāng	l -ín	x -iè
m -èng	d -ù	f -āng

🔘 Read the following words or phrases aloud. Each of them contains a high neutral tone or a low neutral tone. Pay attention to the difference between the high and low neutral tones. Refer to the CD to check your pronunciation.

Low neutral tones:

1) māma (mother)
2) shūshu (uncle)
3) gēge (older brother)
4) jīnzi (gold)
5) xiānsheng (Mister)
6) yéye (grandpa)
7) bóbo (uncles)
8) háizi (children)
9) yínzi (silver)
10) shénme (what)
11) dìdi (younger brother)
12) kàn le (saw)
13) bàba (father)
14) xièxie (thank you)
15) mèimei (younger sister)

High neutral tones:

16) nǎinai (grandma)
17) jiějie (older sister)
18) zuǒ zhe (walking)
19) wǒde (my, mine)
20) nǐde (yours)

Pinyin: Part C

Listen to these country names and then write in the country name in Pinyin with tone marks. Pay special attention to the sounds j, q, x, zh, ch, sh, and r.

1) China_____

2) Hong Kong _____

3) Singapore_____

4) Sweden _____

5) Korea_____

6) Japan _____

7) Switzerland _____

8) Canada _____

9) Spain _____

10) Scotland_____

Listen to these city names, and then put the tone marks over the correct vowel in each word.

1) Xi'an	7) Wulumuqi	13) Changsha
2) Wuhan	8) Shenyang	14) Hangzhou
3) Nanjing	9) Shijiazhuang	15) Taiyuan
4) Guilin	10) Zhengzhou	16) Fuzhou
5) Chengdou	11) Hefei	17) Guangzhou
6) Changchun	12) Nanchang	18) Kunming

▶

19) Guiyang	22) Xining	25) Shenzen
20) Nanning	23) Lasa (Lhasa)	26) Suzhou
21) Lanzhou	24) Yinchua	

Exercise 3

🔘 Read aloud the names of the Chinese provinces, paying special attention to the tones. Refer to the CD to check your pronunciation.

1) Héběi	11) Gānsū	21) Fújiàn
2) Hénán	12) Qīnghǎi	22) Yúnnán
4) Shǎnxī**	13) Xīnjiāng	23) Guǎndōng
3) Shānxī*	14) Sìchuān	24) Guǎngxī
5) Hēilóngjiāng	15) Ānhuī	25) Xīzàng
6) Jílín	16) Húběi	26) Nèiménggu
7) Shāndōng	17) Húnán	27) Běijīng
8) Liáoníng	18) Zhéjiāng	28) Shànghǎi
9) Jiāngsū	19) Jiāngxī	29) Tiājīn
10) Níngxià	20) Guìzhōu	30) Chóngqìng

*sometimes written as "Shanxi"

**sometimes written as "Shaanxi"

Exercise 4

Change the following words so that they use the correct spelling of "i," "u," and "ü" as semi-vowels at the beginning of a syllable.

1) īngguó (England)   4) uǒ (I, me)

2) iángzhōu (a city)   5) üènán (Vietnam)

3) Mr. Uang   6) iě (also) ▶

14

7) xüéxí (to study)
8) uèi (hello)
9) ī (one)
10) üán (¥1.00)

11) iǒu (to have)
12) īn-iáng (the two opposing principles in nature)

Underline each of the initials in the following words.

1) Yǒuyì Shāngdiàn (Friendship Store)

2) Hǎidiàn (a district in Beijing)

3) Gùgōng (Palace Museum)

4) Tiānānmén (Square, Beijing)

5) Tiāntán (Temple of Heaven)

6) Hóngqiáo Shìchǎng (Pearl Market, Beijing)

7) Xiùshuǐ Dōngjiē (Silk Market, Beijing)

8) Yíhéyuán (Summer Palace)

9) Chángchéng (Great Wall)

10) Shísānlíng (Ming Tombs)

11) dàshǐguǎn (embassy)

12) Pānjiāyuán ("Mud Market," Beijing)

Phonetic Systems

In addition to Pinyin, there are two other Chinese phonetic systems still in use today.

Wale-Giles System

The Wade-Giles system is another romanized phonetic system for Chinese. It was created by Thomas F. Wade, who worked at the British embassies in China and Hong Kong from 1841 to 1875. In 1867 he published a Mandarin pronunciation textbook using a romanized phonetic system he devised. Later, another British diplomat, Herbert A. Giles, modified it. The Wade-Giles system was the standard romanization system for spelling Chinese words in English until 1978, when the United Nations adopted Pinyin as the standard.

Chinese National Phonetic Alphabet (CNPA)

The Chinese National Phonetic Alphabet (CNPA) is made up of thirty-nine phonetic marks taken from ancient Chinese characters. It was first issued in 1913 and was adopted by the Chinese Bureau of Education in 1918. It was used in China until 1958, when Pinyin replaced it. It is still used in Taiwan today.

Counting: Part A

🔘 **New Words 1 • 生词一**

Characters	Pinyin	English
数	shǔ	to count
数	shù	number
你	nǐ	you
也	yě	also
我	wǒ	I, me
一	yī	one
二	èr	two
三	sān	three
四	sì	four
五	wǔ	five
加	jiā	to add; plus
六	liù	six
七	qī	seven
八	bā	eight
九	jiǔ	nine
十	shí	ten
是	shì	to be (am, is, are, was, were); yes, correct, right

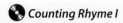 *Counting Rhyme I*

你也数，我也数，
Nǐ yě shǔ, wǒ yě shǔ,

一二三四五。
yī, èr, sān, sì, wǔ.

你也加，我也加，
Nǐ yě jiā, wǒ yě jiā,

四五六七八。
sì, wǔ, liù, qī, bā.

九是四加五。
Jiǔ shì sì jiā wǔ.

十是二加八。
Shí shì èr jiā bā

Translation of Counting Rhyme I

You count, and I count, too:
one, two, three, four, five.
You add, and I add, too:
four, five, six, seven, eight.
Nine is four plus five.
Ten is two plus eight.

🔊 New Words II · 生词二

Characters	Pinyin	English
一百	yìbǎi	one hundred
百	bǎi	hundred
零 (0)	líng	zero
是不是	shì búshì	Is it? / Are they?
不是	búshì	No, it is not.
不	bù	no, not
千	qiān	thousand
万	wàn	ten thousand
亿	yì	billion (hundred million)

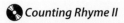 *Counting Rhyme II*

Here is another counting rhyme. This one lets you practice the difficult sounds "s" and "sh" in the words "**sì**," "**shí**," and "**shì**." When you say "**sì**," your tongue is flat and the tip of your tongue touches the lower teeth. When you say "**shí**" or "**shì**," your tongue curls up toward the roof of the mouth, fairly far back. When you say "**sìshí**," your tongue is down and then up. But when you say "**shísì**," your tongue is up and then down. Good luck!

四是四，
Sì shì sì,

十是十。
Shí shì shí.

十四是十四，
Shísì shì shísì,

四十是四十。
Sìshí shì sìshí.

一百是一零零，是不是？
Yìbǎi shì yī líng líng, shì búshì?

Translation of Counting Rhyme II

Four is four,
Ten is ten.
Fourteen is fourteen,
Forty is forty.
One hundred is one-zero-zero, isn't it?

How many terra cotta horses are in this tomb?
Say it in Chinese!

Counting: Part B

The adverb 也 yě (too, also)

也 **yě** is an adverb that functions as a conjunction and must come between the subject and the main verb in a sentence.

你也数，我也数　　　You count, and I count, too.
Nǐ yě shǔ, wǒ yě shǔ.

你也加，我也加　　　You add, and I also add.
Nǐ yě jiā, wǒ yě jiā.

The 是 shì (to be) sentence pattern

是 **shì** is a linking verb that usually connects two nouns, indicating that the nouns on either side of 是 are equal or nominative. For example:

九是四加五　　　Nine is four plus five.
Jiǔ shì sì jiā wǔ.

十是二加八　　　Ten is two plus eight.
Shí shì èr jiā bā.

Especially when stating numbers, you may reverse the sentence order without any change of meaning.

四加五是九　　　Four plus five is nine.
Sì jiā wǔ shì jiǔ.

▶

二加八是十   Two plus eight is ten.
Èr jiā bā shì shí.

Like all Chinese verbs, 是 **shì** does not change, no matter
what the tense, gender, person, or number is. The negative
form of 是 **shì** is 不是 **búshì**.

Affirmative-negative questions with 是不是 *shì búshì (Is it?/Are they?)*

是不是 **shì búshì** is a question that is formed by
combining 是 **shì** (the positive form) with 不是 **búshì**
(the negative form of 是 **shì**). This is an "affirmative-negative" question, which can also be called a "yes-or-no"
question. The answer to it is either the positive form of
是 **shì** (yes) or its negative form 不是 **búshì** (no). For
example:

Q: 一百是一零零，是不是？

　　Yìbǎi shì yī líng líng, shì búshi?
　　One hundred is one-zero-zero, isn't it?

Positive Answer: 是   Yes.
                                  Shì.

Negative Answer: 不是   No.
                                  Búshì.

▶

Any verb can be used in an affirmative-negative question. The answer must be either the affirmative or negative form of the verb in the sentence. For example:

Q: 你数不数数？   Are you counting the numbers?
   Nǐ shǔ bù shǔ shù?

Positive Answer: 数   Yes.
                         Shǔ.

Negative Answer: 不数   No.
                         Bù shǔ.

Counting to 1000

The numbers 0 to 10:

0	零	líng	6	六	liù
1	一	yī	7	七	qī
2	二	èr	8	八	bā
3	三	sān	9	九	jiǔ
4	四	sì	10	十	shí
5	五	wǔ			

Say the numbers 0 to 10 aloud.

The numbers 11–19 follow the pattern 十 **shí** + 1–9:

11	十	+	一	shíyī
12	十	+	二	shí'èr
13	十	+	三	shísān

Say the numbers 11–19 aloud.

The numbers 20–99 follow the pattern 2–9 + 十 **shí** + 1–9:

21	二	+	十	+	一	èrshíyī

34	三	+	十	+	四	sānshísì
42	四	+	十	+	二	sìshí'èr

Say the numbers 20–99 aloud.

The numbers 101–109 follow the pattern 一百 **yìbǎi** + 零 **líng** + 1–9. This is also the pattern for 201–209, 301–309 and so on, all the way up to 901–909:

101	一百	+	零	+	一	yìbǎi líng yī
202	二百	+	零	+	二	èr bǎi líng èr
303	三百	+	零	+	三	sān bǎi líng sān

Say the numbers 101–109 aloud.

If a ten follows a hundred you have to say **yìbǎi yīshí** (110) (not **yìbǎi shí**).

110	一百一十	**yìbǎi yīshí**

The numbers 110–119 follow the pattern

一百 **yìbǎi** + 一十 **yīshí** + 一 **yī** – 十九 **shíjiǔ**.

111	一百	+	一十	+	一	yìbǎi yīshí yī
112	一百	+	一十	+	二	yìbǎi yīshí'èr
113	一百	+	一十	+	三	yìbǎi yīshí sān
114	一百	+	一十	+	四	yìbǎi yīshí sì
115	一百	+	一十	+	五	yìbǎi yīshí wǔ
116	一百	+	一十	+	六	yìbǎi yīshí liù
117	一百	+	一十	+	七	yìbǎi yīshí qī

| 118 | 一百 | + | 一十 | + | 八 | yìbǎi yīshí bā |
| 119 | 一百 | + | 一十 | + | 九 | yìbǎi yīshí jiǔ |

Say the numbers 110–119 aloud.

The numbers 120–199 follow the pattern 一百 **yìbǎi** + 2–9 十 **shí** + 1–9:

120	一百	+	二十			yìbǎi èrshí
121	一百	+	二十	+	一	yìbǎi èrshí yī
122	一百	+	二十	+	二	yìbǎi èrshí èr

Count by tens from 120-190, then count from 190-199.

The numbers 210–1,000 follow the pattern 1–9 + 百 **bǎi** + 一十 **yīshí** + 1–9:

212	二	+	百	+	一十	+	二	èr bǎi yīshí èr
224	二	+	百	+	二十	+	四	èr bǎi èrshí sì
371	三	+	百	+	七十	+	一	sān bǎi qīshí yī
537	五	+	百	+	三十	+	七	wǔ bǎi sānshí qī
699	六	+	百	+	九十	+	九	liù bǎi jiǔshí jiǔ
862	八	+	百	+	六十	+	二	bā bǎi liùshí èr
749	七	+	百	+	四十	+	七	qī bǎi sìshí qī
999	九	+	百	+	九十	+	九	jiǔ bǎi jiǔshí jiǔ
1000	一	+	千					yìqiān

Say the example numbers aloud.

Reading large numbers

To read a large number, starting from the left, for each column say the number, followed by the name of that column.

Note: You do not say the name of the units column, **ge**.

For example, 3,895 shown in the illustration below is read as:

sān qiān	bā bǎi	jiǔshí	wǔ
3,	8	9	5
千	百	十	个
qiān	**bǎi**	**shí**	**gè**
1,000s	100s	10s	units

Try this technique with the following numbers:

3,456   9,872   1,030   5,164   8,927

The 是 shì (to be) sentence pattern

To form a sentence in this pattern, replace the subject and predicate in the example with the groups of words given below.

Subject	*Verb*	*Predicate*
九	是	四加五
Jiǔ	shì	sì jiā wǔ.
Nine	*is*	*four plus five.*
四加五		九
sì jiā wǔ		jiǔ ▶

Subject	Verb	Predicate
二加八 èr jiā bā		十 shí
十 shí		二加八 èr jiā bā
二加一 èr jiā yī		三 sān
五加一 wǔ jiā yī		六 liù
七加四 qī jiā sì		十一 shíyī
我 wǒ		[name]

The affirmative-negative question 是不是 shì búshì

Replace the subject and the predicate in the example with the groups of words given below, then answer the question with either the positive or the negative form of 是 **shì**.

Subject	Affirmative-negative verb	Predicate
一百 Yìbǎi	是不是 shì búshì	一零零？ yī líng líng?
Is one hundred one-zero-zero?		

▶

三加五
Sān jiā wǔ

八
bā

二加二
Èr jiā èr

四
sì

七加九
Qī jiā jiǔ

十六
shíliù

二百加三百
Èr bǎi jiā sān bǎi

五百
wǔ bǎi

你
Nǐ

Lǐ Jiā

Pronunciation Note
Tone Changes

Remember, **yī** (one), **qī** (seven), **bā** (eight), **bù** (no) can each have several different tones.

1. **Yī** can have three different tones.

   A. **Yī** is 1st tone when it is used alone: **yī**, **èr**, **sān**, **sì**, **wǔ**

   B. **Yī** is 2nd tone when followed by a 4th-tone measure word: **yí kuài** (one yuan)

   C. **Yī** is 4th tone when followed by a 1st, 2nd, or 3rd-tone measure word:

yì zhāng (one piece), **yì máo** (one mao), **yì jiǎo** (one jiao), **yì fēn** (one fen)

2. **Qī** and **bā** each can have two tones:
   Qī and **bā** when used alone are 1st tone, but when followed by a 4th-tone measure word, they may change to the 2nd tone:

   qī hào *or* **qí hào** (the number seven)
   bā hào *or* **bá hào** (the number eight)

3. 不 **bù** (no) is 4th tone, except that when it is followed by a 4th tone word, 不 **bù** changes to 2nd tone:
   不是 **búshì** (is not)

Pronunciation Practice

🔘 Practice the tone changes of **yī** (one), **qī** (seven), **bā** (eight), and **bù** (no). Read the following phrases aloud and add the tone marks for **yī**, **qī**, **bā**, and **bù** above the appropriate vowels in the chart below. Check your pronunciaton on the CD.

Pinyin	*Characters*	*English*
a. 1) dìyi	第一	the number one
2) yi tiān	一天	one day
3) yi píng	一瓶	one bottle
4) yi běn	一本	one copy
5) yi gè	一个	one piece
6) yi bēi	一杯	one glass
7) yi wǎn	一碗	one bowl)

8) yi huà	一划	one stroke	
b. 1) dìqi	第七	the seventh	
2) qiyuè	七月	July	
c. 1) dìba	第八	the eighth	
2) bahào	八号	the number eight	
d. 1) bugāo	不高	not tall	
2) buxíng	不行	not okay	
3) buhǎo	不好	not good	
4) bucuò	不错	not bad	
5) buqù	不去	to not go	
6) buxīn	不新	not new	
7) bubì	不必	not necessary	
8) buzǒu	不走	to not leave	

Practice reading aloud the following words with 不 **bù**. Remember that the tone of 不 **bù** changes from 4th to 2nd when followed by a 4th tone. Check your pronunciation on the CD.

Pinyin	*Characters*	*English*
1) bù	不	no
2) duìbùqǐ	对不起	I am sorry.
3) bù zhīdào	不知道	I don't know.
4) tīng bùdǒng	听不懂	I can't understand what you said.
5) bù hǎo	不好	not good
6) bù chī	不吃	to not eat
7) bù lái	不来	to not come

8) búyào	不要	to not want
9) búduì	不对	not correct
10) búcuò	不错	good, not bad at all
11) búxiè	不谢	Not at all. / You're welcome.
12) búkèqi	不客气	You're welcome.

🔘 Read aloud the numbers 0 to 10, organized here by tone.

1st tone	yī (1)	sān (3)	qī (7)	bā (8)
2nd tone	líng (0)	shí (10)		
3rd tone	wǔ (5)	jiǔ (9)		
4th tone	èr (2)	sì (4)	liù (6)	

🔘 Each entry below has an initial sound and a final sound that combine to form complete words. Read the initial and final sound, then read the full word. Check your pronunciation on the audio.

Group A:		Group B:		Group C:		Group D:	
j	iē	z	ū	b	ō	zh	ī
q	iū	c	uī	p	āo	ch	āi
x	iā	s	ūn	m	áng	sh	ān
				f	én	r	ēng

🔊 Read aloud the following words, which have similar sounds.

Group A:

yīshí 一十   yì shí 一石   yímín 移民
yìmíng 译名   yī zì 一字   yǐzi 椅子
yì tiān 一天   yì tián 易田

Group B:

èr zǐ 二子   érzi 儿子   èr nǚ 二女
érnǚ 儿女   èr duǒ 二朵   ěrduo 耳朵

Group C:

sān rén 三人   shànrén 善人   sān diǎn 三点
sǎndiǎn 散点   dàsān 大三   dǎsǎn 打伞

Group D:

sì zhōu 四周   sīchóu 丝绸   sìshū 四书
sǐshù 死树   sìshí 四十   sīshì 私事

Group E:

wǔ tiān 五天   wùtiān 雾天   wǔsì 五四
wúsī 无私   wǔ huí 五回   wùhuì 误会

Group F:

liùshū 六书   liǔshù 柳树   liù píng 六瓶
liūbīng 溜冰   liù jīn 六斤   liúxīn 留心

Group G:

qīshí 七十   qíshì 歧视   qī míng 七名
qǐmíng 起名   qī zhé 七折   qìchē 汽车

Group H:

bābā 八八	bàba 爸爸	bāzì 八字
bǎzi 靶子	bālù 八路	bá shù 拔树

Group I:

jiǔshí 九十	jiùshì 旧事	jiǔjiǔ 九九
jiùjiu 舅舅	jiǔ jīn 九斤	jiūxīn 揪心

Group J:

shí fú 十幅	shīfu 师父	shízì 十字
shìzi 柿子	yīshí 一十	lìshǐ 历史

How many monks are in the temple?
Say it in Chinese!

Using an Abacus

The Chinese abacus has been in use for many hundreds of years. There are two beads that each represent five above the bar and five beads that each represent one below the bar.

By simply extending the process that you have already learned for counting, you can read very large numbers. The columns of an abacus from right to left are **gè** (units), **shí** (tens), **bǎi** (hundreds), **qiān** (thousands), **wàn** (ten thousands), **shíwàn** (hundred thousands), **bǎiwàn** (million), **qiānwàn** (ten million), and **yì** (billion).

yì	qiān wàn	bǎi wàn	shí wàn	wàn	qiān	bǎi	shí	gè
↓	↓	↓	↓	↓	↓	↓	↓	↓
4	7	5,	6	2	3,	4	1	9
亿	千	百	十	万	千	百	十	个
yì	qiān	bǎi	shí	wàn	qiān	bǎi	shí	jiǔ

This is read **sì-yì qī-qiān wǔ-bǎi liù-shí èr-wàn sān-qiān sì-bǎi yīshí jiǔ.**

Start from the left and say the number and then the name of each column, one by one. Notice that you do not say the **wàn** in **qiānwàn**, **bǎiwàn**, and **shíwàn**. You only need to say **qiān**, **bǎi**, **shí**, + **wàn**.

Counting: Part C

🔘 Listen to the numbers on the CD and then write the correct spelling in Pinyin with tone marks for each number in the blanks below.

1) _____
2) _____
3) _____
4) _____
5) _____
6) _____
7) _____
8) _____
9) _____
10) _____

🔘 Listen to these addition problems and write the answers in Pinyin. First study this vocabulary new word:

几 jǐ (how many/much)

Example:

Question: 二加二是几　Èr jiā èr shì jǐ?
How much is two plus two?

Answer: 二加二是四　Èr jiā èr shì sì.
Two plus two is four.

1) _____ 三加六是几？

2) _____ 十加十是几？

3) _____   七加七是几？

4) _____   五十加五十是几？

5) _____   四十五加六十六是几？

🔘 Listen to these
numbers between
11 and 999 and
write them as
Arabic numerals.

1)_____

2)_____

3)_____

4)_____

5)_____

6)_____

7)_____

8)_____

9)_____

10)_____

Exercise 3

Fill in the initial
sound for each
Chinese number.

6: _____ iù   1: _____ ī

7: _____ ī   3: _____ ān

8: _____ ā   5: _____ ǔ

9: _____ iǔ   10: _____ í

Exercise 4

Exercise 5

Add the following symbols and write the sum as a numeral. Then write the problem and the sum in Pinyin, as in the example.

Example: ♦ ♦ ♦ ♦ ♦ + ♦ ♦ ♦ = 8   Wǔ jiā sān shì bā.

1) ♦ ♦ ♦ ♦ + ♦ ♦ ♦ ♦ ♦ = _____

2) ♦ ♦ ♦ ♦ ♦ ♦ ♦ + ♦ ♦ ♦ ♦ ♦ ♦ ♦ =

_____

3) ♦ ♦ ♦ ♦ + ♦ ♦ ♦ ♦ = _____

4) ♦ ♦ ♦ + ♦ ♦ ♦ ♦ ♦ ♦ ♦ ♦ =

_____

5) ♦ ♦ ♦ ♦ ♦ ♦ + ♦ ♦ ♦ ♦ ♦ ♦ ♦ =

_____

6) ♦ ♦ ♦ ♦ ♦ + ♦ ♦ ♦ ♦ ♦ ♦ =

_____

7) ♦ ♦ ♦ ♦ ♦ + ♦ ♦ = _____

Traditional Complex Forms of Numbers

You will notice that Chinese coins and currency have numbers written in the traditional, complex form instead of the modern, simplified form that you have been learning. The complex forms are used in banking (including on checks, payment orders, and receipts) to avoid the problem of someone easily altering 一 **yī** (one) to 十 **shí** (ten) or 千 **qiān** (thousand). Here are the traditional, complex forms of the numbers:

壹 1	貳 2	叁 3	肆 4	伍 5	陸 6
柒 7	捌 8	玖 9	拾 10	佰 100	仟 1000

Some Chinese Superstitions about Numbers

Many Chinese characters are homophones, and so can be puns that suggest another meaning. For example, the pronunciation of **sì** (four) is similar to **sǐ** (death), therefore some people avoid the number four. On the other hand, the pronunciation of **bā** (eight) resembles **fā** (to become rich), so the number eight is a favorite. The numbers **èr bā** (two eight) indicate "two sides become rich." Therefore, in the business world, numbers such as 28; 28,000; 88 and 888 are favorites. In Hong Kong an automobile license plate with the number "888" can be sold for a high price.

Another lucky number is nine. It is an ultimate number in yin-yang philosophy because when yin or yang reaches the value of nine, any further increase will bring it to ten,

▶

where yin turns into yang and where yang turns into yin. Therefore nine represents completeness or fullness in Chinese culture. Nine dragons are a sign of the emperor. Some people use nine in their names.

Chinese also have other lucky associations for numbers, as in "the four kinds of happiness," "the five kinds of luckiness and long life," and "five children reach the summit of achievement."

Money: Part A

🔘 Key Expressions

请问，在哪儿换钱？ Qǐng wèn, zài nǎr huànqián?	Where can I exchange money?
这个多少钱？ Zhè ge duōshao qián?	How much is this?

🔘 New Words 1 · 生词一

Characters	Pinyin	English
你好	nǐ hǎo	Hello! How do you do!
小姐	xiǎojie	Miss, Ms., young lady (used to address female workers in banks, restaurants, stores, hotels, etc.)
小	xiǎo	little, small, young
这个	zhè ge/ zhèi ge	this one, this
这	zhè/zhèi	this
个	gè/ge	(measure word for people or things)

Characters	Pinyin	English
多少	duōshao	How many?, How much?
钱	qián	money
块	kuài	¥1.00 (colloquial form of 元 yuán), dollar
毛	máo	¥0.10 (colloquial form of 角 jiǎo); a surname
那个	nà ge/ nèi ge	that one
那	nà/nèi	that
呢	ne	How about (you, this, that)?
两	liǎng	two
要	yào	to want, would like, need
收	shōu	to accept, to receive
美圆	Měiyuán	U.S. currency, dollar
圆	yuán	¥1.00 (formal written form of 元 yuán), dollar
请	qǐng	please; to invite
问	wèn	to ask

▶

请问	qǐngwèn	May I ask? (Used before asking a question to someone you don't know.)
在	zài	in, at; to be in, to be at, to exist
哪儿	nǎr	Where? (Northern China)
哪	nǎ	Which? What?
换	huàn	to exchange
人民币	Rénmínbì	People's currency (RMB, ¥)
人民	rénmín	people
币	bì	currency, money, coin
中国银行	Zhōngguó Yínháng	Bank of China
中国	Zhōngguó	China
银行	yínháng	bank
谢谢	xièxie	thank you
不谢	búxiè	not at all, you're welcome

🔘 Dialogue I · 对话一

ROLES *A: Foreigner in China* 外国人 ***wàiguórén***;
B: Chinese saleswoman 小姐 ***xiǎojie***

A: 你好！小姐,这个多少钱？
    Nǐ hǎo! Xiǎojie, zhège duōshao qián?

B: 这个一百四十块三毛八。
    Zhèi ge yìbǎi sìshí kuài sān máo bā.

A: 那个呢？
    Nèi ge ne?

B: 那个是一百零八块两毛五。
    Nèi ge shì yìbǎi líng bā kuài liǎng máo wǔ.

A: 我要这个。
    Wǒ yào zhèi ge.

B: 不收美圆。
    Bù shōu Měiyuán.

A: 请问,在哪儿换人民币？
    Qǐngwèn, zài nǎr huàn Rénmínbì?

B: 在中国银行。
    Zài Zhōngguó Yínháng.

A: 谢谢。
    Xièxie.

B: 不谢。
    Búxiè.

Translation of Dialogue I

A: Miss, how much is this?

B: This is 140 kuai, three mao, and eight (fen).

A: How about that one?

B: That one is 108 kuai, two mao, and five (fen).

A: I want this one.

B: I don't accept U.S. dollars.

A: May I ask, where can I exchange for Renminbi?

B: At the Bank of China.

A: Thank you.

B: You're welcome.

The first sentence spoken by the saleswoman is a short form that omits 分 **fēn** at the end of the sentence. The name of the last (smallest) unit of money may be dropped when an amount of money is not a round number. Here is another example:

十块五毛三   ¥10.53
shí kuài wǔ máo sān

Its long form would be:
十块五毛三分 **shí kuài wǔ máo sān fēn** ¥10.53;
an even longer form would be:
十块五毛三分钱
shí kuài wǔ máo sān fēn qián ¥10.53.

🔘 **New Words II · 生词二**

Characters	Pinyin	English
好	hǎo	good, well, OK
元	yuán	¥1.00, dollar
角	jiǎo	¥0.10
分	fēn	¥0.01, cent
外国人	wàiguórén	foreigner
美国人	Měiguórén	American (person)
港币	Gǎngbì	Hong Kong dollar (HK$)
外币	wàibì	foreign currency
这儿	zhèr	here
那儿	nàr	there
兑换单	duìhuàndān	exchange form
签字	qiānzì	to sign, to affix a signature

🎧 Dialogue II · 对话二

ROLES *A: American* 美国人 *Měiguórén;*

B: Bank clerk/teller 小姐 *xiǎojie*

A: 你好! 小姐,我换人民币。
   Nǐ hǎo! Xiǎojie, wǒ huàn Rénmínbì.

B: 你好! 请问你换多少钱?
   Nǐ hǎo! Qǐng wèn nǐ huàn duōshao qián?

A: 我换一百美圆。
   Wǒ huàn yìbǎi Měiyuán.

B: 好。
   Hǎo.

A: 这是多少人民币?
   Zhè shì duōshao Rénmínbì?

B: 这是八百二十元两角六分。
   Zhè shì bā bǎi èrshí yuán liǎng jiǎo liù fēn.

A: 谢谢。
   Xièxie.

A: 不谢。
   Búxiè.

Translation of Dialogue II

A: How do you do! Miss, I want to exchange for Renminbi.

B: How do you do! May I ask, how much do you want to exchange?

A: I want to exchange 100 dollars.

B: OK.

A: How much is this in Renminbi?

B: This is 820 yuan, two jiao, and six fen.

A: Thank you.

B: You're welcome.

Money: Part B

The question word 多少 duōshao (how many, how much)

多少 **duōshao** usually comes after the verb. Notice that this is unlike the word order of English. An exception is when 多少 **duōshao** forms an independent sentence such as 多少钱？ **Duōshao qián?** (How much money?) or 多少人？ **Duōshao rén?** (How many people?).

Q: 这是多少钱？ How much is this?
Zhè shì duōshao qián?

A: 这是一百美圆。 This is 100 dollars.
Zhè shì yìbǎi Měiyuán.

The question word 呢 ne (how about, what about, where is)

呢 **ne** is a modal particle that is used at the end of a sentence. Here it is used to make a question:

那个呢？ How about that one?
Nà ge ne?

小姐呢？ Where is the saleswoman?
Xiǎojie ne?

二 èr (two) and 两 liǎng (two)

Both 两 **liǎng** and 二 **èr** mean *two*, but they have different uses:

a. 两 **liǎng** is the quantity two (a cardinal number)

两个人	liǎng ge rén	two people
两块钱	liǎng kuài qián	two kuài
两层楼	liǎng céng lóu	two floors
两瓶啤酒	liǎng píng píjiǔ	two bottles of beer
两个门	liǎng ge mén	two doors

b. 二 **èr** is for the second in a sequence (an ordinal number)

二层	èrcéng	second floor
二楼	èrlóu	second floor; second building
二门	èrmén	second door
二号	èrhào	second day of the month; number two
二班	èrbān	second group

There are a few words that may use either **liǎng** or **èr**:

Two kilos, which is a quantity, may be either 两斤 **liǎng jīn** or 二斤 **èr jīn**.

Two máo, which is a quantity, may be either 两毛 **liǎng máo** or 二毛 **èr máo**

▶

c. The number 2 is 二 **èr** (not 两 **liǎng**) in 12, 20–29, 32, 42 up to 92 and 102, 202, etc.

---

d. When the number 2 is in 200, 2,000, 20,000, etc., you may use either 两 **liǎng** or 二 **èr**. The northern and the southern Chinese have different preferences. For example:

	Northern	Southern
200	两百 liǎng bǎi	二百 èr bǎi
2,000	两千 liǎng qiān	二千 èr qiān
20,000	两万 liǎng wàn	二万 èr wàn

在 zài (be in/at) + place name

在 **zài** as a preposition (in, at) is always followed by a place word to form a prepositional phrase and means *to be in or at some place.*

在哪儿换钱？	(At) where (can I)
Zài nǎr huànqián?	exchange money?

在银行换钱。	(You can) exchange money
Zài yínháng huànqián.	at the bank.

In Chinese the "**zài** + place" prepositional phrase must always come before the verb:

Subject + ***zài*** + *place* + *verb* + *object*

我在银行换钱。   I exchange money at the bank.
Wǒ zài yínháng huànqián.

Notice that the Chinese word order is different from English, which can have "in the bank" at the end of the sentence.

The question word 哪儿 *nǎr (where)*

哪儿 **nǎr** is an interrogative pronoun that is often used with the preposition 在 **zài** (in, at) to ask questions. When you ask the question *Where is …?*, the pattern is:

在 *zài* + 哪儿 *nǎr* + *Verb* + *Object*

在	哪儿	换	钱？	Where can I
Zài	nǎr	huàn	qián?	exchange money?

Units of money

Review the formal and colloquial terminology for money. Remember to be consistent in using either the formal or the colloquial usage, without mixing them.

	Units	Tenths	Hundredths
Formal Usage	元	角	分
	yuán	jiǎo	fēn
Colloquial Usage	块	毛	分
	kuài	máo	fēn

The following chart shows some examples of how to say an amount of money. Just insert the number before the name of its unit. For example:

	Formal			*Colloquial*		
¥1.32	1元	3角	2分	1块	3毛	2
	yí yuán	sān jiǎo	èr fēn	yí kuài	sān máo	èr
¥4.55	4元	5角	5分	4块	5毛	5
	sì yuán	wǔ jiǎo	wǔ fēn	sì kuài	wǔ máo	wǔ

	Formal		Colloquial	
¥6.70	6元	7角	6块	7
	liù yuán	qī jiǎo	liù kuài	qī
¥189.00	189元		189块	
	yìbǎi bāshí jiǔ yuán		yìbǎi bāshíjiǔ kuài	

Asking questions with 多少 duōshao

Practice using 多少 **duōshao,** *how many/how much,* to form questions. Fill in the chart below using the subjects and objects provided. The first one is done for you.

Question				Answer			
Subj.	*Verb*	*Int.*	*Object*	*Subj.*	*Verb*	*No.*	*Object*
这	是	多少	钱？	这	是	一百	美元。
Zhè	shì	duō-shao	qián?	Zhè	shì	yìbǎi	Měi-yuàn.
How much money is this?				*This is $100.*			
那	duō shao		人民币	那	shì	300	RMB
nà			Rénmínbì	nà			
这			美元	这		150	US$
zhè			Měiyuàn	zhè			
那			港币 (HK$)	那		500	HK$
nà			Gǎngbì	nà			
这			块	这		1,000	块
zhè			kuài	zhè			kuài

那		元	那	95	元
nà		yuán	nà		yuán
这		钱	这	200	块钱
zhè		qián	zhè		kuài qián

Asking questions with 呢 *ne*

Form a question by adding 呢 **ne** at the end of a sentence.

Subject	*Verb*	*Object*	*Subject*	*Particle*
这	是	一百块,	那个	呢?
Zhè	shì	yìbǎi kuài,	nà ge	ne?

This is 100 kuai, how about that one?

Practice this using the subjects, verbs and objects provided.

我		[your name]	你
wǒ			nǐ
我		美国人	你
wǒ		Měiguórén	nǐ
我	要	这个	你
wǒ	yào	zhè ge	nǐ
我	换	钱	你
wǒ	huàn	qián	nǐ

The number two

Practice the number two. When two precedes a measure word, use 两 **liǎng** (not 二 **èr**).

Number	*Measure word*	*Noun*
两	块	钱。
Liǎng	kuài	qián.
	角	人民币
	jiǎo	Rénmínbì
	百	港币
	bǎi	Gǎngbì
	分	钱
	fēn	qián
	美元	
	Měiyuàn	

Where?

Use the pattern "**zài** + **nǎr** + Verb + Object" to ask *Where is...?*

Question				Answer	
Qǐngwèn	***zài* + *nǎr***	*Verb*	*Object*	***Zài***	*Location*
请问	在哪儿	换	钱？	在	中国银行。
Qǐng wèn	zài nǎr	huàn	qián?	Zài	Zhōngguó Yínháng.

May I ask, where can I exchange money?

At the Bank of China.

美元	这儿
Měiyuàn	zhèr
人民币	那儿
Rénmínbì	nàr
港币	中国银行
Gǎngbì	Zhōngguó
	Yínháng

Pronunciation Note
Tone changes: 3+3 → 2+3

Whenever a 3rd tone is followed by another 3rd tone, the first one changes to a 2nd tone. For example:

wǔ jiǎo 五角	→	wú jiǎo	five **jiao**
xǐzǎo 洗澡	→	xízǎo	to take a bath
shěngzhǎng 省长	→	shéngzhǎng	provincial governor
zǒngtǒng 总统	→	zóngtǒng	a nation's president

When three or more 3rd tones are in succession, all except the last one change to 2nd tones. For example:

Wǒ hěn hǎo. 我很好。   →   Wó hén hǎo.
I am very well.

Wǒ yě hěn hǎo. 我也很好。 →   Wó yé hén hǎo.
I am very well, too.

Pronunciation Practice

Read the following numbers and words aloud, paying special attention to the tone combinations in each.

Pinyin	Characters	English
1) Nǐ hǎo!	你好!	Hello!
2) hěn hǎo	很好	very good
3) Běihǎi	北海	the North Sea
4) bǔkǎo	补考	make-up test
5) hǎidǎo	海岛	island
6) shuǐjiǎo	水饺	dumpling
7) xiǎojie	小姐	Miss

8) bǎoxiǎn	保险	insurance
9) lǎoshǔ	老鼠	mouse
10) zuǒshǒu	左手	left hand
11) qǐdǎo	祈祷	to pray
12) lǎohǔ	老虎	tiger
13) qǐngtiē	请贴	invitation
14) Wǒ xiǎng xǐzǎo.	我想洗澡。	I want to take a bath.
15) zǒngtǒngfǔ	总统俯	the office building of the president

💿 Read the following numbers and words aloud in Chinese, paying special attention to the tone combinations in each. Check your pronunciation on the CD.

1) 1999	2) 1959	3) 1995	4) 9595
5) 5959	6) 6845	7) 9059	8) 3737
9) 2000	10) 2001	11) cèsuǒ	12) Xīmén
13) sìjiào	14) sháoyuán	15) qīhàolóu	

💿 Each entry below has an initial sound and a final sound that combine to form complete words. Read the initial sound and the final sound, then read the full word. Check your pronunciation on the CD.

Group A:		Group B:		Group C:		Group D:	
g	uàn	j	iāng	d	é	b	ǎng
k	àn	q	īng	t	ái	p	ěng
h	ào	x	uān	l	iáo	m	ěi
				n	ú	f	ǎn

🔊 Read the following numbers and words aloud in Chinese, paying special attention to the tone combinations in each. Check your pronunciation on the CD.

1) Niǔyuē (New York)
2) Wòtàihuá (Ottawa)
3) Bōshìdùn (Boston)
4) Mèngfēisī (Memphis)
5) Luòshānjī (Los Angeles)
6) Jiùjīnshān (San Francisco)
7) Fèichéng (Philadelphia)
8) Huáshèngdùn (Washington, D.C.)
9) Bālí (Paris)
10) Lúndūn (London)
11) Wéiyěnà (Vienna)
12) Bólín (Berlin)
13) Āmǔsītèdān (Amsterdam)
14) Huìlíndùn (Wellington)

Money: Part C

🔘 Read and listen to the following dialogue and then answer the questions:

> *A: Foreigner* 外国人 *wàiguórén;*
> *B: Bank clerk* 小姐 *xiǎojie;*

A: 小姐, 我要换钱。

B: 你要换多少?

A: 我要换两百美圆的人民币。

B: 好。

A: 这是两百美圆。

B: 这是一千六百六十块人民币。

A: 谢谢。

B: 不谢。再见。

A: 再见。

Questions:

1. What did the foreigner want to do?_____

_____

2. What kind of currency and what amount did he want to exchange at the bank? _____

_____

3. What amount did he receive? _____

_____

4. How many RMB equal one U.S. dollar? _____

_____

🔘 Read and listen to the dialogue and then answer the questions.

> A: Foreigner 外国人 *wàiguórén*;
> B: Bank clerk 小姐 *xiǎojie*;

A: 小姐,这个多少钱？

B: 这个两百块。

A: 那个呢？

B: 那个两块五。

A: 我要那个。

B: 好。

A: 谢谢!

B: 不谢。再见。

A: 再见。

Questions:

1. Which item did the American want? _____

_____

2. How much did he pay the clerk? _____

_____

3. What did the clerk say after he gave her the money? ___

_____

Exercise 3

All the words for RMB units of money are measure words. Practice using 两 **liǎng**, *two*, with the units of money given. Write them in Pinyin and read them aloud.

1. ¥2.00 块

2. ¥0.02 分

3. ¥222.00 元

4. ¥2000 千

5. ¥2.20 毛

6. ¥200 百

7. ¥0.20 角

8. $2.00 美元

Exercise 4

Write the following numbers in Pinyin and read them aloud.

37	_____	56	_____
94	_____	27	_____
19	_____	65	_____
12	_____	73	_____
100	_____	109	_____
123	_____	176	_____

Chinese Currency

There are thirteen denominations of bills and six coins that make up the Chinese currency. The bills are 100 yuán, 50 yuán, 20 yuán, 10 yuán, 5 yuán, 2 yuán, 1 yuán, 5 jiǎo, 2 jiǎo, 1 jiǎo, 5 fēn, 2 fēn, and 1 fēn. The coins are 1 yuán, 5 jiǎo, 1 jiǎo, 5 fēn, 2 fēn, and 1 fēn. The dimensions of paper currency and of coins are scaled to their denominations, from largest to smallest.

Exchange in China

Foreign currency can be exchanged at most major banks, international airports, some large hotels, some large department stores, and some tourist areas. You need to show your passport or a foreign resident's ID. The exchange rate varies slightly from one place to another, and a slightly more favorable rate is given for traveler's checks. Be sure to keep the receipt when you exchange money because you will need those receipts in order to convert RMB back to foreign currency. It is illegal to exchange foreign currency on the street, and you are likely to be given counterfeit money if you do. Foreign credit cards can also be used to obtain RMB from Chinese ATMs but you can expect to pay a fee for the transaction.

At a Cafeteria: Part A

🎵 Key Expressions

您要什么菜？ Nín yào shénme cài?	What dishes would you like to order?
我要这个菜。 Wǒ yào zhè ge cài.	I want this dish.
我还要酸辣汤。 Wǒ hái yào suān làtāng.	I also want hot-and-sour soup.
这是牛肉吗？ Zhè shì niúròu ma?	Is this beef?
不要了，谢谢！ Bú yào le, xièxie.	I don't want any more, thank you!

🎵 New Words 1 · 生词一

Characters	*Pinyin*	*English*
食堂	shítáng	cafeteria
吃饭	chīfàn	to eat a meal
吃	chī	to eat
饭	fàn	meal; cooked rice
吗	ma	(forms a question)

很	hěn	very, very much
您	nín	you (polite form)
什么	shénme	What?
菜	cài	dish, vegetable
牛肉	niúròu	beef
牛	niú	cow
肉	ròu	meat (When combined with the word for an animal, means a specific type of meat. When used alone, often implies "pork".)
猪肉	zhūròu	pork
猪	zhū	pig
米饭	mǐfàn	cooked rice
馒头	mántou	steamed bread, steamed bun
还	hái	in addition, still, yet
了	le	(indicates a change of situation or completed action)

🔘 **Dialogue I · 对话一**

ROLES *A: Customer* 顾客 *gùkè;*

B: Server 服务员 *fúwùyuán*

A: 你好吗?
    Nǐ hǎo ma?

B: 我很好, 您呢?
    Wǒ hěn hǎo, nín ne?

A: 我也很好。
    Wǒ yě hěn hǎo.

B: 您要什么菜?
    Nín yào shénme cài?

A: 我要这个菜。这个菜是 牛肉 吗?
    Wǒ yào zhè ge cài. Zhè ge cài shì niúròu ma?

B: 不是 , 是猪肉。那个是牛肉。
    Búshì, shì zhūròu. Nà ge shì niúròu.

A: 我要那个菜。
    Wǒ yào nà ge cài.

B: 您要米饭吗?
    Nín yào mǐfàn ma?

A: 不要,我要馒头。
    Bú yào, wǒ yào mántou.

B: 还要什么?
    Hái yào shénme?

▶

A: 不要了。谢谢!
    Bú yào le. Xièxie!

B: 不谢!
    Búxiè!

Translation of Dialogue I

A: How are you?

B: I am fine, and you?

A: I am also fine.

B: What [dishes] would you like to order?

A: I want this one. Is it beef?

B: No, it is pork. That one is beef.

A: I'll have that dish.

B: Would you like rice?

A: No, I would like steamed bread.

B: Anything else?

A: No, thank you.

B: You're welcome.

New Words II · 生词二

Characters	Pinyin	English
你们	nǐmen	you (plural)
有	yǒu	to have
鸡	jī	chicken
鱼	yú	fish
都	dōu	all, both Adverb: never used to describe a noun
汤	tāng	soup
鸡蛋汤	jīdàntāng	egg-drop soup
鸡蛋	jīdàn	egg
和	hé	and
酸辣汤	suānlàtāng	hot-and-sour soup
酸	suān	sour
辣	là	spicy, hot
面条	miàntiáo	noodles
饼	bǐng	fried bread

🔵 **Dialogue I · 对话二**

ROLES *A: Customer* 顾客 *gùkè;*
B: Server 服务员 *fúwùyuán*

A: 请问, 你们有什么菜?
Qǐng wèn, nǐmen yǒu shénme cài?

B: 鸡, 鱼, 肉都有。
Jī, yú, ròu dōu yǒu.

A: 我要一个鸡, 一个鱼。
Wǒ yào yí ge jī, yí ge yú.

B: 要不要汤?
Yào búyào tāng?

A: 你们有什么汤?
Nǐmen yǒu shénme tāng?

B: 鸡蛋汤和酸辣汤。
Jīdàntāng hé suānlàtāng.

A: 要一个鸡蛋汤。
Yào yí ge jīdàntāng.

B: 还要什么?
Hái yào shénme?

A: 还要一个面条, 一个饼。谢谢!
Hái yào yí ge miàntiáo, yí ge bǐng. Xièxie!

B: 不谢。
Búxiè.

Translation of Dialogue II

A: May I ask, what dishes do you have?

B: Chicken, fish, and meat (dishes): we have all of them.

A: I want one chicken dish and one fish (dish).

B: Would you like soup?

A: What kinds of soup do you have?

B: We have egg-drop soup and hot-and-sour soup.

A: I'd like an egg-drop soup.

B: Anything else?

A: I also want one (order of) noodles and one (order of) fried bread. Thank you.

B: Not at all.

At a Cafeteria: Part B

The question word 么 ma

吗 **ma** is added to the end of an affirmative sentence to make a yes-or-no question. It is the most commonly used form of question in Chinese. 吗 **ma** is always a neutral tone.

这个菜是牛肉吗？   Is this dish a beef dish?
Zhè ge cài shì niúròu ma?

The question word 什么 shénme (what)

什么 **shénme** is an adverb that functions as a conjunction and must come between the subject and the main verb in a sentence.

您要什么   What do you want? / What
Nín yào shénme?   would you like to order?

什么 **shénme** can also be put at the beginning of a sentence:

什么是"牛肉"？   What is "niúròu"?
Shénme shì "niúròu"?

The particle 了 *le*

了 **le** is an important particle in Chinese, and it has several functions. 了 **le** in the previous dialogues serves two functions, which can occur separately or simultaneously:

1) In Chinese, an action or event has an "aspect," independent of whether it occurs in the past, present, or future. The "aspect" of an action or event is its current situation, such as "in progress" or "completed". 了 **le** following a verb indicates the action is completed or the event is concluded. Notice that 了 **le**, as an aspect particle, does not indicate past or present tense, even though "verb + 了 **le**" often refers to an action that took place in the past.

2) 了 **le** at the end of a sentence indicates a change of situation or that a new situation has occurred. An example from dialogue 1 in lesson 10 is "不要了 **búyào le** No thank you (Meaning "I don't want to order any more.")

了 **le** can occur after the verb and also at the end of the sentence, serving both functions together. It shows that the action associated with "I want" is completed and that "I don't want any more" is a new situation.

(In a negative sentence these functions are accomplished by using a negative adverb 没 **méi** or 没有 **méiyǒu** before the verb. 了 **le** is not used.)

我吃了。 Wǒ chī le.	I have eaten. [the action of eating is over]
我没(有)吃。 Wǒ méi (yǒu) chī.	I haven't eaten.

The adverb 都 dōu *in a topic-comment sentence*

鸡，鱼，肉都有 **Jī, yú, ròu dōu yǒu** (Chicken, fish, and meat: we have all of them).

In this sentence, the topic is 鸡，鱼，肉 **jī, yú, ròu**, and the comment is 都有 **dōu yǒu**. The real subject, 我们 **wǒmen** (we), is skipped. The topic-comment structure is a very common sentence pattern in Chinese.

Affirmative-negative questions (with any verb)

You have already seen the affirmative-negative question with 是不是 **shì búshì** (yes or no?). Affirmative-negative questions can be formed with any verb. 要不要 **yào búyào** (do you want) is an affirmative-negative question formed by combining the positive form of the verb (要 yào) with the negative form of the verb (不要 **búyào**). The answer is simply either the positive or the negative form of the verb. For example:

Q: 你要不要米饭？ Do you want rice?
    Nǐ yào búyào mǐfàn?

A: 要。 Yes.   or   不要。 No.
    Yào.   Búyào.

The particle 吗 *ma*

The particle 吗 **ma** is used at the end of a sentence to turn a statement into a question.

Subject	*Verb/Adj*	*Object*	*ma*
这个菜	是	牛肉	吗？
Zhè ge cài shì	niúròu		ma?

Is this a beef dish?

Practice asking questions with the question word 吗 **ma** and the subjects, verbs and objects below.

那 Nà	猪肉 zhūròu	
你 Nǐ	要 yào	鸡蛋汤 jīdàntāng
你们 Nǐmen	有 yǒu	馒头 mántou
你 Nǐ	换 huàn	钱 qián
你 Nǐ	好 hǎo	
那个菜 Zhè ge cài	辣 là	

The question word 什么 shénme (what)

A. Practice making new sentences with 什么 **shénme:**

Question			Answer		
Subj.	*Verb*	*Int.*	*Subj.*	*Verb*	*Object*
您	要	什么?	我	要	牛肉。
Nín	yào	shénme?	Wǒ	yào	niúròu.

What would you like to order? I want beef.

	吃				面条
	chī				miàntiáo
	吃				面条
	chī				miàntiáo
	有			有	鸡和鱼
	yǒu			yǒu	jī hé yú
	还要			还要	米饭
	hái yào			hái yào	mǐfàn
	有	什么汤		有	酸辣汤
	yǒu	shénme tāng		yǒu	suānlàtāng
	换	什么钱		换	美元
	huàn	shénme qián		huàn	Měiyuán

▶

B. Now practice asking questions with 什么 shénme at the beginning of a sentence:

Question			Answer		
Subj.	*Verb*	*Object*	*Subj.*	*Verb*	*Object*
什么	是	"牛肉"?	"牛肉"	是	beef.
Shénme	shì	"niúròu"?	"Niúròu"	shì	beef.
What is "niúròu"?			*"Niúròu" is beef.*		
		馒头	馒头		steamed bread
		mántou	mántou		
		饼	饼		fried bread
		bǐng	bǐng		
		面条	面条		noodles
		miàntiáo	miàntiáo		
		人民币	人民币		中国钱
		Rénmínbì	Rénmínbì		Zhōngguó qián
		一元	一元		十个角
		yì yuán	yì yuán		shí ge jiǎo
		港币	港币		HK$
		Gǎngbì	Gǎngbì		

The particle 了 le

The particle 了 **le** at the end of a sentence or after a verb indicates the "aspect" of an action that is completed. To answer a question with 了 **le**, use the pattern "不 **bú** … 了 **le**" (not … any more) which indicates a change of situation.

Practice asking questions with the question word 吗 **ma** and answering with 了 **le**:

Question				*Answer*		
Subj.	***hái*** *+verb*	*object*	**ma**	*Negative of Verb* + *le*		
你	还要	菜	吗？	不	要	了。
Nǐ	hái yào	cài	ma?	Bú	yào	le.
Would you like		*more dishes?*		*(I) don't want any more.*		
	还吃	米饭			吃	
	hái chī	mǐfàn			chī	
	还要	这个菜			要	
	hái yào	zhè ge cài			yào	
	还吃	鱼			吃	
	hái chī	yú			chī	
	还要	汤			要	
	hái yào	tāng			yào	
	还吃	面条			吃	
	hái chī	miàntiáo			chī	

Affirmative-negative questions

An affirmative-negative question can be formed with any verb. Practice asking questions with this pattern and answering in both the affirmative and the negative.

Question		*Answer*
Verb in Affirmative-Negative	*Object*	*Affirmative Answer/ Negative Answer*
要不要 Yào búyào	这个菜？ zhè ge cài?	要。/ 不要。 Yào. / Búyào.
Would you like this dish?		*Yes, I would. / No, I wouldn't.*
	米饭 mǐfàn	要馒头 / 不要米饭 Yào mántou. / Búyào mǐfàn.
	这个菜 zhè ge cài	要那个菜 / 不要这个菜 Yào nà ge cài. / Búyào zhè ge cài.
	汤 tāng	要菜 / 不要汤 Yào cài. / Búyào tāng.
	面条 miàntiáo	要饼 / 不要面条 Yào bǐng. / Búyào miàntiáo.
	猪肉 zhūròu	要牛肉 / 不要猪肉 Yào niúròu. / Búyào zhūròu.
	鱼 yú	要鸡 / 不要鱼 Yào jī. / Búyào yú.

Questions with 还要 *hái yào (to still want, to want more)*

Use the following words to make new sentences with this pattern.

Question				Answer		
Subj.	***Hái*** + *Verb*	*Object*	***Ma***	***Hái*** + *Verb*		*Object*
你	还要	汤吗？		还	要	酸辣汤。
Nǐ	hái yào	tāng	ma?	Hái	yào	suānlà-tāng.

Do you want more soup?   *Yes, (I) want more hot-and-sour soup.*

菜	那个菜
cài	nà ge cài
米饭	米饭
mǐfàn	mǐfàn
面条	鸡蛋面
miàntiáo	jīdànmiàn

吃	吃	面条和饼
chī	chī	miàntiáo hé bǐng
吃肉	吃	牛肉
chī ròu	chī	niúròu

Pronunciation Note
Tonal modification:
The half-3rd tone at the beginning

When a 3rd tone is by itself it is pronounced as a full 3rd tone. But when a 3rd tone is at the beginning of a word or compound and is followed by a different tone (1st, 2nd, or 4th tone), the 3rd tone is pronounced as a half-3rd tone, which falls but does not rise. The printed tone mark does not change. For example, in the following compounds, **měi** is pronounced as a short, half 3rd tone.

Pinyin	*Chinese*	*English*
měi tiān	每天	every day
měi nián	每年	every year
měi yuè	每月	every month

Pronunciation Practice

Read the following words and phrases with initial 3rd tones aloud.

Pinyin	*Characters*	*English*
1) wǒ chī	我吃	I eat
2) wǒ lái	我来	I will come
3) wǒ yào	我要	I want
4) nǐ hē	你喝	you drink
5) nǐ lái	你来	you will come
6) nǐ huàn	你换	you change
7) wǔ tiān	五天	five days
8) wǔ nián	五年	five years
9) wǔ cì	五次	five times
10) lǎoshī	老师	teacher

Practice these words that have 3rd tones followed by 2nd tones.

Pinyin	*Characters*	*English*
1) Měiguó	美国	United States
2) lǎorén	老人	old person
3) zhǎoqián	找钱	give change
4) gǎigé	改革	to reform
5) hǎiyáng	海洋	ocean
6) yěmán	野蛮	barbarous
7) jiǎngtái	讲台	platform
8) zǒngcái	总裁	company president
9) jiějué	解决	to solve
10) jǐngchá	警察	police

 Each entry below has an initial sound and a final sound that combine to form complete words. Read the initial and the final sound, then read the full word. Check your pronunciation on the audio.

Group A:	Group B:	Group C:	Group D:
zh ē	d uō	z ài	g uāi
ch áo	t ú	c án	k uí
sh ǎng	l iǎo	s uān	h é
r ì	n àn		

 Practice Pinyin by reading the following terms aloud.

1) xuéxiào 学校 school
2) xiǎoxué 小学 elementary school
3) zhōngxué 中学 secondary school
4) dàxué 大学 university, college

5) Jiàoyùbù 教育部 Ministry of Education
6) Jiàoyùjú 教育局 Bureau of Education
7) Zhōngyāng Zhèngfǔ 中央政府 Central Government
8) shěng 省 province
9) Guówùyuàn 国务院 State Council
10) shì 市 city
11) xiàn 县 county
12) Shāngyèbù 商业部 Ministry of Commerce
13) shāngdiàn 商店 store
14) Nóngyèbù 农业部 Ministry of Agriculture
15) nóngcūn 农村 countryside
16) Wénhuàbù 文化部 Ministry of Culture
17) chāojí shìchǎng 超级市场 / chāoshì 超市 supermarket
18) shūdiàn 书店 bookstore
19) zǎoshì 早市 morning market
20) jǐngchájú 警察局 police bureau
21) pàichūsuǒ 派出所 police station
22) gōngsī 公司 company
23) lǜshīsuǒ 律师所 law firm
24) yóujú 邮局 post office
25) yīwùsuǒ 医务所 clinic
26) yīyuàn 医院 hospital
27) bàngōngshì 办公室 office
28) lǚguǎn 旅馆 / fàndiàn 饭店 / bīnguǎn 宾馆 hotel
29) gōngyuán 公园 park
30) zhàoxiàngguǎn 照相馆 photo shop

At the Cafeteria: Part C

🔘 Read and listen to the dialogue below, and then answer the questions.

First review these new vocabulary words:

碗 wǎn (bowl)

找 zhǎo (to give change back)

AT A COUNTER 在柜台

> A: Foreigner 外国人 **wàiguórén**;
> B: Server 服务员 **fúwùyuán**

A: 你要什么？

B: 我要一个馒头。

A: 还要什么？

B: 还要一碗米饭。多少钱？

A: 三块钱。

B: 这是五块钱。

A: 找你两块钱。

B: 好，谢谢。

Questions:

1. What does the foreigner ask for first? _____

   _____

2. What else does the foreigner ask for? _____

   _____

▶

3. How much is the total cost?_____

_____

4. The change the foreigner receives back is _____

_____

🔘 Listen to the dialogue and answer the questions. First review the word that is not in the vocabulary list for this lesson:

一共 yígòng (altogether, in total)

A: 我要这个菜。这个菜多少钱？

B: 这个菜两块五。

A: 那个菜多少钱？

B: 那个菜三块钱。

A: 我要一个这个菜，一个那个菜。

B: 好，一共五块五。

Questions:

1. How many dishes does the foreigner order? _____

2. How much is the total bill? _____

Exercise 3

Practice ordering these dishes, saying: "我要 **Wǒ yào** _____."

菜 cài
鸡 jī
鱼 yú
牛肉 niúròu
米饭 mǐfàn
馒头 mántou

Exercise 4

Write the names of the following foods in Pinyin in the blanks.

1. fish   _____

2. chicken   _____

3. noodles   _____

4. beef   _____

Exercise 5

To prepare to buy food at a cafeteria in China, translate these sentences into Chinese. Write your answers in Pinyin.

1. Is this a beef dish? _____

2. I don't want this dish. I want that dish. _____

3. I would like egg-drop soup._____

_____

▶

4. I also want four steamed buns. _____

_____

5. I don't want any more, thank you. _____

_____

Terms for Waiter or Waitress

服务员 **fúwùyuán** is the general term for waiters and waitresses. However a waiter is usually referred to as 师傅 **shīfu** and a waitress as 小姐 **xiǎojie**. But be alert for regional usage—in some places, especially in the south, 小姐 **xiǎojie** has a slang meaning of "call girl," and the term for a waitress is 小妹 **xiǎomèi** ("little sister").

Shítáng 食堂 (Cafeteria)

Almost all work places in China have a 食堂 **shítáng**, which is a cafeteria or dining hall, including a "faculty cafeteria" (教师食堂 **jiàoshī shítáng**) at schools or an "employee cafeteria" (职工食堂 **zhígōng shítáng**) at government agencies, companies, and other working places. The word 食堂 **shítáng** usually indicates a style of food service in which you stand in line and choose food you see behind a counter. The servers then will give you the food, and you carry it to your seat. Coupons, sold at a counter or in an office in or near the cafeteria, are often used instead of cash. Chinese colleges usually have a separate foreigners' cafeteria called 留学生食堂 **liúxuéshēng shítáng** (foreign students' cafeteria) for all foreigners including students, teachers and other visitors. Foreigners are expected to eat there instead of at the regular cafeteria for Chinese people. Foreign students' cafeterias usually sell both Chinese-style food and Western-style food.

Banquets and Family Dinners

A foreign guest in China sometimes has the change to attend banquets. Those banquets have different levels of formality, according to the rank of the host. As the rank of the host increases, the etiquette becomes more complex.

At a very ceremonial banquet the hosts will formally meet the guests before the banquet in a reception hall. The seating arrangement depends on the rank of the hosts and guests, but name cards are usually placed at the tables.

There are usually three glasses in front of each person: a small glass for **Máotái** (a well-known brand of strong liquor), a stemmed glass for wine, and a glass for water or soft drinks. The host gives the first toast, usually with wine, instead of the higher alcohol-content **Máotái**, to symbolize friendship. At a formal banquet only the highest-ranking host will go around to the other tables to toast. All the other people should stay at their table and toast only the people at that table. When toasting, your glass should be held a little lower than the other person's to show your respect.

A finger towel will be offered three times during the banquet for you to clean your hands. The first time is when you sit down. The second time is after eating greasy foods and soup. The third time is at the end of the banquet.

If you are invited to the home of a friend or colleague for dinner, you should take a gift (fruit, wine, flowers, candy, cake, or toys for children). The etiquette at a family dinner is less formal than at a banquet. The host might ask you to sit at a special place or simply have you sit wherever you choose. A finger towel might be offered to clean your hands before, during or after the meal, or there might only be napkins. There will likely be formal toasts before the dinner begins. The host will usually take some food from the dishes on the table and put it on your plate. It is impolite to refuse to eat it.

At a Restaurant: Part A

🔘 *Key Expressions*

你们有什么菜？ Nǐmen yǒu shénme cài?	What dishes do you have?
我吃素。有素菜吗？ Wǒ chīsù. Yǒu sùcài ma?	I am a vegetarian. Do you have vegetarian dishes?
小姐！买单。 Xiǎojie! Mǎidān.	Waitress! The check, please.
一共多少钱？ Yígòng duōshao qián?	How much is it altogether?

🔘 *New Words 1* · 生词一

Characters	*Pinyin*	*English*
饭馆(儿)	fànguǎn(r)	restaurant
进	jìn	to enter, to come in
这边	zhèbian	this side, over here
边	biān	side, edge

坐	zuò	to sit
美国人	Měiguórén	American (person)
我们	wǒmen	we, us
英国人	Yīngguórén	British person
(一)点儿	(yì)diǎnr	a little; some
菜单	càidān	menu
来	lái	to bring; to come, to arrive
炒	chǎo	to stir-fry
炒鸡丁	chǎojī-dīng	stir-fried diced chicken with diced vegetables
鸡丁	jīdīng	diced chicken
丁	dīng	cube, diced piece
糖	táng	sugar, sweets, candy
醋	cù	vinegar
糖醋	tángcù	sweet-and-sour (things)
片	piàn	slice, thin piece
葱	cōng	green onion

爆	bào	to quick-fry, to explode
葱爆	cōngbào	quick-fried with green onion
没	méi	not; to not have (short form of 没有 méiyǒu)
没有	méiyǒu	to not have
先	xiān	first; before
这些	zhèxie	these
些	xiē	some, a few, a little

💿 **Dialogue I · 对话一**

ROLES *A: Customer* 顾客 **gùkè**;
B: Waitress/waiter 小姐 **xiǎojie**/师傅 **shīfu**

B: 请进。请这边坐。
Qǐng jìn. Qǐng zhèbian zuò.

A: 谢谢。
Xièxie.

B: 你们是美国人吗？
Nǐmen shì Měiguórén ma?

A: 不是。我们是英国人。
Búshì. Wǒmen shì Yīngguórén.

B: 你们吃点儿什么？
    Nǐmen chī diǎnr shénme?

A: 你们有什么菜？
    Nǐmen yǒu shénme cài?

B: 这是菜单。
    Zhè shì càidān.

A: 好。来一个炒鸡丁，一个糖醋鱼片，一个酸
    辣汤。有没有葱爆牛肉？
    Hǎo. Lái yí ge chǎojīdīng, yí ge tángcù yúpiàn, yí
    ge suānlàtāng. Yǒu méiyǒu cōngbào niúròu?

B: 没有。
    Méiyǒu.

A: 先要这些。谢谢。
    Xiān yào zhèxie. Xièxie.

Translation of Dialogue I

B: Please come in. Please sit here.

A: Thank you.

B: What would you like to order?

A: What dishes do you have?

B: Here is the menu.

A: OK. Please bring one stir-fried diced chicken, one
    sweet-and-sour sliced fish, and one hot-and-sour
    soup. Do you have quick-fried beef with green
    onions?

B: No.

A: I'll have these first. Thank you.

请 **qǐng** (please, to invite) is used in the dialogue before the main verb of an imperative sentence in order to be polite.

请进。	Qǐng jìn.	Come in, please.
请坐。	Qǐng zuò.	Sit down, please.

请 **qǐng** can also be used alone to politely invite people to come in, sit down, eat or drink, etc., according to the context.

请! 请!	Qǐng. Qǐng.	Please [sit down]. Please [have more].
请多来点儿。	Qǐng duō lái diǎnr.	Please have more.

这边 **zhèbian** (on this side) (or **zhèbianr** in Beijing) is a place word that usually comes before the verb in a sentence. You can also put 在 **zài** as a preposition before the place word without any change of meaning:

请这边坐。
Qǐng zhèbian zuò.   Please sit on this side.

请在这边坐。
Qǐng zài zhèbian zuò.   Please sit on this side.

一个炒鸡丁,	一个糖醋鱼片
yí ge chǎojīdīng	yí ge tángcù yúpiàn
one stir-fried diced chicken	one sweet-and-sour sliced fish

The measure word 个 **ge**, as a generic measure word for many objects, can be used for ordering food dishes in a restaurant. Otherwise 盘 **pán** is the measure word for food dishes.

New Words II • 生词二

Characters	Pinyin	English
吃素	chīsù	vegetarian; to eat only vegetables
素	sù	plain; vegetable
素菜	sùcài	vegetable dish
炒鸡蛋	chǎojīdàn	scrambled eggs
喝	hē	to drink
饮料	yǐnliào	drinks, beverages
茶	chá	tea
咖啡	kāfēi	coffee
冷饮	lěngyǐn	cold drink(s)
啤酒	píjiǔ	beer
杯	bēi	cup, glass
可乐	kělè	cola (short for 可口可乐 Kěkǒu Kělè)
水	shuǐ	water
瓶	píng	bottle
买单	mǎidān	bill/check (in a restaurant or bar only)

一共	yígòng	altogether, in total
杯子	bēizi	cup
盘子	pánzi	plate
碗	wǎn	bowl
筷子	kuàizi	chopsticks
勺子	sháozi	spoon
叉子	chāzi	fork
宫保	gōngbǎo	a spicy, diced meat dish

💿 Dialogue II · 对话二

ROLES *A: Customer* 顾客 *gùkè*;
          B: Waitress 小姐 *xiǎojie*

A: 我吃素。有素菜吗？
    Wǒ chīsù. Yǒu sùcài ma?

B: 有炒鸡蛋，炒素菜。
    Yǒu chǎojīdàn, chǎosùcài.

A: 我要一个炒素菜。
    Wǒ yào yí ge chǎosùcài.

B: 你们喝什么饮料？
    Nǐmen hē shénme yǐnliào?

A: 你们有什么？
    Nǐmen yǒu shénme?

B: 茶，咖啡，冷饮和啤酒都有。
    Chá, kāfēi, lěngyǐn hé píjiǔ dōu yǒu.

A: 要两杯可乐，一杯水，一瓶啤酒。
    Yào liǎng bēi kělè, yì bēi shuǐ, yì píng píjiǔ.

        * * *

A: 小姐！买单。一共多少钱？
    Xiǎojie! Mǎidān. Yígòng duōshao qián?

B: 一共一百二十五块。
    Yígòng yìbǎi èrshíwǔ kuài.

A: 谢谢。
    Xièxie.

Translation of Dialogue II

A: I am a vegetarian. Do you have vegetarian dishes?

B: We have scrambled eggs and stir-fried vegetable dishes.

A: I want to order a stir-fried vegetable dish.

B: What would you like to drink?

A: What kind of drinks do you have?

B: We have tea, coffee, cold drinks, and beer.

A: We'd like two glasses of cola, one glass of water, and one bottle of beer.

      * * *

A: Miss! The check, please. How much is the total?

B: Altogether it is 125 yuan.

A: Thank you.

没有 **méiyǒu** (to not have) is the only negative form of 有 **yǒu** (to have). Notice that 不 **bù** is never used with 有 **yǒu**.

At a Restaurant: Part B

The adverb (一) 点儿 (yì) diǎnr

点儿 **diǎnr** (a little) usually follows a verb to indicate "doing something a little." 吃点儿什么? **Chī diǎnr shénme?** (What would you like to eat?) literally means *What would you like to eat a little?* 点儿 **diǎnr** is a shortened form of 一点儿 **yìdiǎnr** (a little) with 一 **yì** (a) omitted; it modifies 什么 **shénme** (what) in the example above.

Sentences with subjects omitted

In Chinese the subject of a sentence can often be omitted when the context makes clear who or what the subject is.

A: 有素菜吗?   Do you have vegetarian dishes?
   Yǒu sùcài ma?

B: 有。 Yes, we do.
   Yǒu.

The adverb 一共 yígòng

The adverb 一共 **yígòng** (altogether, in total) is used only with numbers and must be put immediately before the number.

一共一百二十五块。 Altogether 125 yuan.
Yígòng yìbǎi èrshíwǔ kuài.

What would you like to eat?

吃点儿什么？ **Chī diǎn shénme?** (What would you like to eat?) is a very common first question for a server to ask a customer in a Chinese restaurant.

Question				Answer		
Subj.	Verb	**diǎnr**	Int.	Subj.	Verb	Object
你们	吃	点儿	什么？	我	要	炒鸡丁。
Nǐmen	chī	diǎnr	shénme?	Wǒ	yào	chǎojīdīng.

What would you like to eat?   *I would like stir-fried diced chicken.*

Practice asking and answering questions with this pattern using the verbs and objects provided.

Subj.	Verb	**diǎnr**	Int.	Subj.	Verb	Object
	喝				喝	水
	hē				hē	shuǐ
	要				要	糖醋鱼
	yào				yào	tángcùyú
	来				来个	炒鸡蛋
	lái				lái ge	chǎojīdàn

You can add information after 什么 **shénme** to make the question more specific. For example: 你们吃点儿什么菜？ **Nǐmen chī diǎnr shénme cài?** (What dishes would you like to eat?)

▶

Practice asking and answering questions with this pattern:

Question				Answer		
Subj.	Verb	**diǎnr**	Int.	Subj.	Verb	Object
	喝	什么饮料?			要	可乐
	hē	shénme yǐnliào?			yào	kělè
	要	什么菜?			来个	素菜
	yào	shénme cài			lái ge	sùcài

Do you have …?

有 **Yǒu** …吗 **ma?** (Do you have …?) is a sentence pattern with the subject omitted. It is used very often in restaurants, shops, and markets.

Yǒu	*Object*	**ma**
有	咖啡	吗?
Yǒu	kāfēi	ma?

Do you have coffee?

The negative answer to this question is
没有。 **Méiyǒu.** (No, I don't have …)

Practice making new sentences with this pattern using the objects provided:

米饭
mǐfàn

葱爆牛肉
cōngbào niúròu

炒素菜
chǎo sùcài

茶
chá

面条
miàntiáo

Do you have …?

有没有 **Yǒu méiyǒu** …? (Do you have …?) is an affirmative-negative question. It is formed by combining the positive verb 有 **yǒu** with the negative verb 没有 **méiyǒu**. The answer can be either 有 **yǒu** (yes, to have) or 没有 **méiyǒu** (no, to not have). This question form is frequently used in daily life in China. The meaning of 有没有 **Yǒu méiyǒu** …? is the same as 有 **Yǒu** …吗 **ma**?

有没有　　素菜？	有。 / 没有。
Yǒu méiyǒu sùcài?	Yǒu. / Méiyǒu.
Do you have vegetarian dishes?	*Yes, we do. / No, we don't.*

Practice asking and answering questions with this pattern using the objects provided.

Object	*Answer*
可乐 kělè	no
汤面 tāngmiàn	yes
炒鸡蛋 chǎojīdàn	no
牛肉 niúròu	yes
啤酒 píjiǔ	no
炒肉丁 chǎoròudīng	yes

What do you have?

有什么 **Yǒu shénme** ...? (What do you have?) can be used to ask what kinds of food you can order.

Question				Answer		
Subject	*Verb*	*Int.*	*Object*	*Subject*	*Verb*	*Object*
你们	有	什么	菜?	我们	有	鸡,鱼,肉。
Nǐmen	yǒu	shénme	cài?	Wǒmen	yǒu	jī, yú, ròu.

Practice asking and answering questions using this pattern with the objects provided below.

Object: Question	*Object: Answer*
鸡 jī	炒 鸡丁 chǎojīdīng
<u>鱼</u> yú	糖醋鱼 tángcùyú
肉 ròu	葱爆牛肉 cōngbào niúròu
菜 cài	炒素菜 chǎosùcài
啤酒 píjiǔ	美国啤酒 Měiguó píjiǔ
饮料 yǐnliào	可乐 和水 kělè hé shuǐ

How much is it?

Use 一共 **yígòng** to ask how much the bill is, and then answer with the amount.

Question		Answer	
Total is	Int.	Total is	Number
一共	多少钱？	一共	三十五 块。
Yígòng	duōshao qián?	Yígòng	sānshíwǔ kuài.
			¥15.50
			¥7.25
			¥133.40
			¥54.30
			¥200
			¥10.12

Pronunciation Note
The letter "e"

There are two pronunciations of the letter "e": the central vowel and the high front vowel.

1. The central vowel pronunciation is like the pronunciation of "*uh*," where the lips are spread and sound is coming from the throat. Be sure to spread your lips instead of rounding them, which is the common tendency when English speakers first try to pronounce this sound.

The central vowel pronunciation is used when "e" occurs in the following three instances:

a. "e" alone as an independent syllable

Pinyin	Chinese	English
Éguó	俄国	Russia
Wǒ è le.	我饿了。	I am hungry.

b. "e" as the final of a syllable

Pinyin	Chinese	English
hé	河	river
chē	车	vehicle, car
wǒde	我的	mine, my
Déguó	德国	Germany
Dézhōu	德州	Texas

c. "e" in the final "en" or "eng"

Pinyin	Chinese	English
Ēn	恩	kindness, grace
gēn	根	root, end
zhēn	真	real
dēng	灯	light
zhēng	蒸	to steam

2. The high front vowel "e" pronunciation is like the American English pronunciation of "hay." It is used when "e" is in a diphthong.

Pinyin	Chinese	English
měi [like English "may"]	美	beautiful
hēi [like English "hay"]	黑	black
bēizi	杯子	cup
Chūnjié	春节	the Spring Festival

Pronunciation Practice

🔊 Read the following words aloud. Be careful to pronounce the central vowel "e" and the front high vowel "e" correctly.

"e" alone as an independent syllable:

1) Éguo	俄国	Russia
2) ézi	蛾子	moth
3) étou	额头	forehead
4) Wǒ è le.	我饿了。	I am hungry.

"e" as the final of a syllable:

5) shé	蛇	snake
6) kuàilè	快乐	happy
7) qìchē	汽车	automobile
8) zhèngcè	政策	policy
9) Huánghé	黄河	the Yellow River
10) tèkuài	特快	express train
11) Kěkǒu Kělè	可口可乐	Coca-Cola®
12) Déguó	德国	Germany
13) Dézhōu	德州	Texas
14) Búkèqi	不客气	You are too polite. / You're welcome.

"e" in the final "en" or "eng":

15) shén	神	god, deity, divinity
16) mén	门	door
17) Ménggǔ	蒙古	Mongolia
18) mèng	梦	dream
19) hěn hǎo	很好	very good
20) néng	能	can, able to

"e" in a diphthong:

21) mèimei	妹妹	younger sister
22) gěi	给	to give
23) Běijīng	北京	Beijing
24) zéi	贼	thief
25) jiějie	姐姐	older sister
26) tiělù	铁路	railway
27) zhédié	折叠	to fold
28) dǎliè	打猎	to hunt

🔘 Here are more words that contain the vowel "e". Read them aloud, being careful to pronounce the central vowel "e" and the front high vowel "e" correctly.

Pinyin	Chinese	English
1) xiǎojie	小姐	Miss
2) hē shuǐ	喝水	to drink water
3) wǔ fēn	五分	five fen
4) Měiguó	美国	America

▶

5) gēge	哥哥	older brother
6) Éhàiě	俄亥俄	Ohio
7) xiǎofèi	小费	tip
8) huǒchē	火车	train
9) cèsuǒ	厕所	restroom
10) fēng	风	wind
11) shéngzi	绳子	rope

💿 Each entry below has an initial sound and a final sound that combine to form complete words. Read the initial and final sounds separately, then read the full word. Check your pronunciation on the audio.

Group A:	Group B:	Group C:	Group D:
b ēi	zh è	j iǔ	z ài
p ō	ch ǎo	q iàn	c ōng
m án	sh í	x iāng	s ù
f áng	r éng		

💿 Read the following names of fruits and vegetables aloud.

1) guā 瓜 melon, squash

2) guǎnggān 广柑 grapefruit

3) kǔguā 苦瓜 bitter gourd

4) kōngxīncài 空心菜 a hollow stemmed green vegetable

5) huángguā 黄瓜 cucumber

6) húluóbù 胡萝卜 carrot

▶

7) yángcōng 洋葱 onion

8) yángbáicài 洋白菜 cabbage

9) wāndòu 豌豆 peas

10) wōsǔn 莴笋 Chinese asparagus

11) zhīmá 芝麻 sesame

12) zhúsǔn 竹笋 bamboo shoots

13) cándòu 蚕豆 broad bean

14) càihuā 菜花 cauliflower

At a Restaurant: Part C

🔘 Listen to the dialogue below, then answer the questions.

First study this new vocabulary word:

羊肉 yángròu (lamb)

A: Customer 顾客 **gùkè**;

B: Waiter 师傅 **shīfu**

B: 请进，请这边坐。

A: 谢谢。

B: 您吃点儿什么？

A: 你们有什么菜？

B: 鸡，鱼，肉都有。

A: 你们有什么肉？

B: 有猪肉，牛肉，羊肉。

A: 我要一个羊肉。

Questions:

1. What did the customer ask the waiter first? _____

_____

2. What did the customer ask the waiter after that? _____

_____

3. What did the customer finally order? _____

_____

🔘 Listen to the dialogue, then answer the questions.

First study these new vocabulary words:

茶 chá (tea)   壶 hú (pot)

　A: Customer 顾客 **gùkè**;

　B: Waiter 师傅 **shīfu**

B:　您喝什么？

A:　你们有什么？

B:　我们有啤酒，有汽水。

A:　我不要啤酒。有茶吗？

B:　有茶。

A:　我要一壶茶。

Questions:

1. What did the waiter ask the customer? _____

_____

2. What beverage did the waiter offer? _____

_____

3. What did the customer want? _____

_____

Exercise 3

It's your turn to order a meal in Chinese! Choose three dishes that you would like to order from the menu below. Tell the waiter/waitress what you would like, then ask how much it will cost.

Example:

A. Waiter/waitress:　　你们吃点儿什么？
　　　　　　　　　　　Nǐmen chī diǎnr shénme?

B. Customer:　　　　　来一个 …
　　　　　　　　　　　Lái yí ge….
　　　　　　　　　　　一共多少钱？
　　　　　　　　　　　Yígòng duōshao qián?

菜单 MENU

素菜 Sùcài

炒素菜 chǎosùcài	¥6.00
炒鸡蛋 chǎojīdàn	¥5.00
素烧豆腐 sùshāo dòufu	¥7.00

肉菜 Ròucài

葱爆牛肉 cōngbào níuròu	¥16.00
炒鸡丁 chǎojīdīng	¥14.00
炒三丁 chǎosāndīng	¥12.00
炒肉片 chǎoròupiàn	¥18.00

You are about to go to dinner at a Chinese restaurant with some friends. To prepare, translate the following sentences into Chinese. Write them in Pinyin or characters.

1. What dishes do you have? _____

_____

2. Two of us are vegetarians. Do you have vegetarian dishes?

_____

_____

3. Please bring us two glasses of beer, one cola and one water. (来 **lái** bring) _____

_____

4. We would like to order three dishes: one quick-fried beef with onions, one fish and one vegetable dish. _

_____

_____

_____

5. Miss, the check please. How much is it altogether? (一共 **yígòng** altogether)_____

_____

Tips (小费 xiǎofèi)	There is traditionally no tipping in Chinese restaurants. However, restaurants in top-level hotels now often add a 15 percent service charge to the bill.

Types of Food in China

The two basic categories of restaurants are Chinese-style (中餐 **zhōngcān**) and Western-style (西餐 **xīcān**). There are many Chinese restaurants named after local cuisine. For instance, "Peking duck" (北京烤鸭 **Běijīng kǎoyā**) restaurants serve dishes made with duck roasted over an open fire. "Sichuan-style" (四川风味 **Sìchuān fēngwèi**) restaurants serve spicy food from Sichuan. "Guangdong-style" (粤菜 **Yuècài**) or **Gǎngcài** (港菜 **Gǎngcài** Hong Kong–style) restaurants serve dimsum and other specialties from Guangdong and Hong Kong. There are also vegetarian restaurants in large cities in China. A Western-style restaurant usually serves both European and American food. 韩国烧烤 **Hánguó shāokǎo** restaurants sell Korean barbecue and food, and 日本料理 **Rìběn liàolǐ** restaurants serve Japanese cuisine. 家常菜 **jiā cháng cài** means *family style*, and those restaurants usually serve northern-style food.

Phone Calls: Part A

 Key Expressions

怎么给美国打电话？ Zěnme gěi Měiguó dǎdiànhuà?	How do I make a call to the United States?
请告诉她给我回电话。 Qǐng gàosu tā gěi wǒ huí diànhuà.	Please tell her to call me back.
您贵姓？ Nín guì xìng?	What's your surname?
我姓…/我叫… Wǒ xìng…/Wǒ jiào…	My surname is…/My full name is…
您的电话是多少号？ Nínde diànhuà shì duō shǎo hào?	What's your phone number?

New Words 1 · 生词一

Characters	Pinyin	English
怎么	zěnme	how, in what way
给	gěi	to; for (when transferring something to someone); to give

美国	Měiguó	United States
打	dǎ	to make (a phone call); to hit, to beat; to play (ball)
电话	diànhuà	telephone
打电话	dǎ diànhuà	to make a phone call
拨	bō	to dial (a rotary phone)
再	zài	again, still
地区	dìqū	area, region
号	hào	number, code, size
分	fēn	minute
分钟	fēnzhōng	minute
钟	zhōng	clock, o'clock
太	tài	too, excessively, extremely
贵	guì	expensive, valuable, honored
用	yòng	to use
电话卡	diànhuàkǎ	telephone card

卡	kǎ	card
买	mǎi	to buy
邮局	yóujú	post office
商店	shāngdiàn	shop, store
商	shāng	business; a surname/ last name
店	diàn	shop, store
卖	mài	to sell

🔘 Dialogue I · 对话一

ROLES *A: Foreigner* 外国人 *wàiguórén;*

　　　　B: Attendant 服务员 *fúwùyuán*

A: 请问, 怎么给美国打电话?
　　Qǐng wèn, zěnme gěi Měiguó dǎ diànhuà?

B: 先拨 0 0 1, 再拨地区号和电话号。
　　Xiān bō líng líng yāo[1], zài bō dìqūhào hé diàn-
　　huàhào.

A: 多少钱 一分钟?
　　Duōshǎo qián yì fēnzhōng?

B: 八块。
　　Bā kuài.

A: 太贵了。
　　Tài guì le.

B: 用电话卡不太贵。两块四一分钟。
　　Yòng diànhuàkǎ bú tài guì. Liǎng kuài sì yì
　　fēnzhōng.

A: 在哪儿买?
　　Zài nǎr mǎi?

B: 邮局和商店都卖。
　　Yóujú hé shāngdiàn dōu mài.

1. The number "1" in a telephone number (or a street address, etc.) is often
　 pronounced **yāo** rather than **yī**.

Translation of Dialogue I

A: Excuse me, how can I make a phone call to the United States?

B: First dial 001, and then dial the area code and the number.

A: How much is it per minute?

B: Eight yuan.

A: That's too expensive.

B: It is not too expensive to use a phone card. (It's) two yuan and forty fen per minute.

A: Where can I buy one?

B: At the post office or in stores.

打电话 **dǎ diànhuà** is the only way in Chinese to say *to make a phone call*; it is a "verb + object" construction. 打 **dǎ** is a verb with the primary meaning of *to hit* or *to beat*, but it is also widely used in "verb + object" constructions for actions such as *to make a call*, *to buy a ticket*, or *to play ball*.

拨 **bō** (to dial) means *to dial a rotary telephone*:

先拨 001。 First dial 001.
Xiān bō líng líng yāo.

If the telephone has push buttons, it's better to say 按 **àn** (to press):

请先按 001。   Please first dial 001.
Qǐng xiān àn líng líng yāo.

分钟 **fēnzhōng** (minute)

分 **fēn** is a unit of time and means *minute*. 钟 **zhōng** is
a noun that means *clock* or, as here, *time according to the
clock*. 一分钟 **yì fēnzhōng** is *one minute*. 分 **fēn** as a unit
word is also used for money; for example, 一分钱 **yì fēn
qián** is *one fen*.

卡 **kǎ** is a phonetic translation of *card*. It is added to
some other words to form new nouns, such as 信用卡
xìnyòngkǎ (credit card), 提款卡 **tíquǎnkǎ** (debit card) or
卡片 **kǎpiàn** (name card). 卡 **kǎ** is also a phonetic translation of *car*, as in 卡车 **kǎchē** (truck).

🔘 New Words II · 生词二

Characters	Pinyin	English
新	xīn	new, fresh
园	yuán	garden
宾馆	bīnguǎn	hotel, guesthouse
喂	wèi	hello (used on the tele-phone or to get someone's attention)
找	zhǎo	to look for, to seek; to give change (also, "I want to speak to …")

谁	shéi/shuí	Who?
房间	fángjiān	room
的	de	(function word)
她	tā	she, her
告诉	gàosu	to tell, to inform, to let know
回	huí	to return, to go back
贵姓	guì xìng	Your surname, please?
姓	xìng	to be surnamed; surname, family name
叫	jiào	to be called, to call out
您的	nínde	yours (polite form)
你的	nǐde	yours (informal)
我的	wǒde	my, mine
不客气	búkèqi	You're welcome.
新园宾馆	Xīnyuán Bīnguǎn	Xinyuan Hotel

马丽莎   Mǎ Lìshā (name of a person)

护照   hùzhào   passport

🔊 Dialogue II · 对话二

ROLES *A: Foreigner* 外国人 *wàiguórén;*

B: Hotel attendant 服务员 *fúwùyuán*

A:　喂,是新园宾馆吗?
　　Wèi, shì Xīnyuán Bīnguǎn ma?

B:　是 , 您找谁?
　　Shì, nín zhǎo shéi?

A:　我找314房间的马丽莎。
　　Wǒ zhǎo sān yāo sì fángjiān de Mǎ Lìshā[1].

B:　她不在。
　　Tā bú zài.

A:　请告诉她给我回电话。
　　Qǐng gàosu tā gěi wǒ huí diànhuà.

B:　请问您贵姓?
　　Qǐng wèn, nín guì xìng?

A: 我姓商,叫商美英。
   Wǒ xìng Shāng, jiào Shāng Měiyīng.

B: 您的电话是多少号?
   Nínde diànhuà shì duōshǎo hào?

A: 我的电话是 6725–4831。谢谢!
   Wǒde diànhuà shì liù qī èr wǔ–sì bā sān yāo.
   Xièxie!

B: 不客气。
   Búkèqi.

1 丽莎 **Lìshā** is the Chinese pronunciation of "Lisa."

Translation of Dialogue II

A: Hello. Is this the Xinyuan Hotel?

B: Whom are you calling?

A: I am looking for Ma Lisha in room 314.

B: She is not in.

A: Please tell her to call me back.

B: What's your surname?

A: My surname is Shang and my full name is Shang Meiying.

B: What is your number?

A: My number is 6725–4831. Thank you.

B: You're welcome.

她 **tā** (she)
In modern Chinese, the pronoun 她 **tā** means *she* and the pronoun 他 **tā** means *he*. Traditionally, however, all pronouns in Chinese were gender neutral.

她 **tā** is a new character that was created only in the twentieth century when Chinese intellectuals wanted to translate *she* from Western languages. Many people still write 他 whether referring to a man or a woman.

Saying telephone numbers
In China you should say each digit in a phone number separately. For instance, 800 is said "eight, zero, zero" (*not "eight hundred"*), and 3159 is said as "three, one, five, nine" (*not "thirty-one, fifty-nine"*). Remember that in reading a telephone number, "1" is often pronounced **yāo** rather than **yī**.

Telephone Cards

Two basic kinds of phone cards in China are called "IC" cards and "IP" cards. "IC" phone cards are accepted only by special public phones called **cíkǎ diànhuà** (magnetic phones). The cost is the same as other public phones, with a service fee for long distance calls. You can buy an IC card at post offices, department stores and large hotels. You cannot use an IC card to make calls at home or in a hotel room.

"IP" phone cards or "200" phone cards can be used to make calls at home and in hotel rooms. They can be used for both local and long-distance calls. They are much cheaper for international calls than any other method. You can buy them in stores, at post offices, and in hotel business centers. Before you use the card you must scratch off the covering from the code number. On the next page, you can see a typical 200 (IP) phone card. Here is a translation of the instructions on the back of a typical card.

How to make a phone call:

- Pick up the phone and dial 200

- Dial (1) for Mandarin Chinese; (2) for Cantonese; (3) for English

- Enter card number

- Enter code number

- Dial (1) for long distance; (2) to check balance of minutes; (3) to change code number

- Hang up

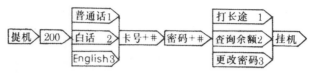

使用方法   有效期 95.12.31

说明:

1.保密处理:请您挂机后重新提机按任一键
2.按 * 键可取消输错的卡号或密码
3.语言选择后,可不听提示语直接操作
4.全省联网后异地使用时卡号为17550 + 现有卡号
5.遗忘密码处理:请拨电话9686800208

咨询电话:8818272 9686800200

The back of a typical IC, or 200, phone card.

Phone Calls: Part B

The interrogative 怎么 *zěnme (how)*

怎么 **zěnme** (how) is an interrogative adverb that is used to ask the manner or method of an action. 怎么 **zěnme** must be located before the main verb of the sentence:

怎么换钱？ Zěnme huàn qián?	How do I exchange money?
这个怎么卖？ Zhè ge zěnme mài?	How do you sell this? How is this sold?

If there is a prepositional phrase before the main verb, 怎么 **zěnme** should be placed before the preposition:

怎么给美国打电话？ Zěnme gěi Měiguó dǎ diànhuà?	How can I make a phone call to the United States?

The preposition 给 *gěi (to, toward)*

In the phrase 给美国打电话 **gěi Měiguó dǎ diànhuà** (make a phone call to the United States), 给 **gěi** (to, toward) is a preposition in the phrase 给美国 **gěi Měiguó** and is located before the main verb 打 **dǎ**. In this context, 给 **gěi** can introduce either a place or a person:

给中国打电话 gěi Zhōngguó dǎ diànhuà	to make a call to China

▶

给北京打电话   to make a call to Beijing
gěi Běijīng dǎ diànhuà

给你打电话   to call you
gěi nǐ dǎ diànhuà

先 xiān … 再 zài … (first … then)

先 **xiān**… 再 **zài**… is used to describe two actions or
events in succession. 先 **xiān** is for the first action or
event; 再 **zài** is for the second:

先买电话卡，再打电话。   Buy a phone card first, (and)
Xiān mǎi diànhuàkǎ,   then make phone calls.
zài dǎ diànhuà.

太 tài … 了 le (too, excessively, extremely …)

太 **tài** is an adverb that modifies an adjective or a verb,
and is used to express degree or extent. It must be placed
immediately before that adjective or verb. 太 **tài** … 了 **le** is
a frame that can take any adjective. For example:

太好了! Tài hǎo le!   It's great!

太多了! Tài duō le!   It's too much!

太客气了! Tài kèqi le!   (You're) too polite!

If an adjective is commendatory (positive), as in the above
examples, the 了 **le** is required. However, if the adjective
is derogatory you can simply put 太 **tài** before it, and the
了 **le** is optional. For example, both 太贵了 **tài guì le** (too
expensive) and 太贵 **tài guì** (too expensive) are
acceptable.

The particle 的 *de*

的 **de** is a function word that has many different uses in Chinese. You will learn two functions of 的 **de** in this lesson.

a. 的 **de** as a modifier marker:

的 **de** occurs very frequently after a word, a phrase, or a clause to form a 的 **de** phrase that modifies a noun. 的 **de** is used like the English *who*, *which*, or *that*.

我找314房间的马丽莎。   I am looking for Ma Lisha
Wǒ zhǎo sān yāo sì fángjiān   who is in room 314.
de Mǎ Lìshā.

b. 的 **de** shows possession:

Adding 的 **de** after a pronoun or noun makes a possessive form.

您的 nínde	yours (polite form)
我的 wǒde	my; mine
你的 nǐde	yours
那是我的，不是你的。 Nà shì wǒde, búshì nǐde.	That is mine, not yours.

在 *zài (to be in/at) as a verb*

马小姐在吗？ **Mǎ Xiǎojie zài ma?** is a standard expression that means *Is Miss Ma in?* in which 在 **zài** is used as a verb and no place word follows it. The place word is omitted because the context makes clear that the place is 这儿 **zhèr** (here) or 那儿 **nàr** (there). The negative answer is 她不在 **Tā bú zài**. (She is not in [here/there]).

You have already learned 在 **zài** as a preposition. You can identify 在 **zài** as a preposition, rather than a verb, when there is a main verb in the sentence and when 在 **zài** is followed by a place word: 在 **zài** + place word + verb. Here is an example of 在 **zài** as a preposition:

我在银行换钱。   I exchange money in the bank.
Wǒ zài yínháng huàn qián.

您贵姓？ *Nín guì xìng? (What's your surname?)*

您贵姓？ **Nín guì xìng?** (What's your surname?) is the polite way of asking a surname, and it is a fixed expression, especially when using 您 **nín** (you), the polite form of 你 **nǐ**. 贵 **guì** usually means *expensive*, but here means *honorable*, modifying 姓 **xìng** (surname). 您贵姓 **Nín guì xìng?** (What's your surname?) is understood as a question and does not have an interrogative word.

The reply will be: 我姓 … **Wǒ xìng** … (My surname is …)

姓 *xìng (to be surnamed; a surname)*

Usually 姓 **xìng** acts as a verb. Thus in a question 姓 **xìng** is followed by 什么 **shénme** (what), and in the answer it is followed by a Chinese surname:

您姓什么？   What is your surname?
Nín xìng shénme?

我姓商。   My surname is Shang.
Wǒ xìng Shāng.

The negative form is 不姓 **bú xìng**:

我不姓商;我姓张。   I am not surnamed Shang; I am
Wǒ bú xìng Shāng; wǒ   surnamed Zhang.
xìng Zhāng.

Sometimes 姓 **xìng** can act as a noun that means "surname":

欧阳是我的姓   Ouyang is my surname.
Ōuyáng shì wǒde xìng.

How

怎么 **zěnme** (how) must be before the main verb. If there is a prepositional phrase before the main verb, 怎么 **zěnme** must be placed before the preposition. For example: 怎么给美国打电话？ **Zěnme gěi Měiguó dǎ diànhuà?** (How can I make a phone call to the United States?)

Practice making interrogative sentences with 怎么 **zěnme**:

Zěnme	*Verb*	*Object*
怎么	打	电话？
Zěnme	dǎ	diànhuà?

How do I make phone calls?

	换	钱
	huàn	qián
	买	电话卡
	mǎi	diànhuàkǎ
	炒	鸡丁
	chǎo	jīdīng
	买	饭票
	mǎi	fànpiào (meal ticket)
	用	这个
	yòng	zhè ge
	要	买单
	yào	mǎidān

First ... then

先 **xiān** ...再 **zài** (first ... then) is used to arrange two actions or events in succession. 先 **xiān** introduces the first action or event, and 再 **zài** introduces the second. Practice making new sentences with this structure.

Xiān	*Verb*	*Object*	***zài***	*Verb*	*Object*
先	拨	地区号，	再	拨	电话号。
Xiān	bō	dìqūhào,	zài	bō	diànhuàhào.

First dial the area code, (and) then dial the telephone number.

买	电话卡，		打	电话
mǎi	diànhuàkǎ,		dǎ	diànhuà
拨	0 0 1，		拨	10
bō	línglíngyāo,		bō	yī líng
换	人民币，		买	饭票
huàn	Rénmínbì,		mǎi	fànpiào
找	你，		找	马丽莎
zhǎo	ní,		zhǎo	Mǎ Lìshā
喝	啤酒，		吃	饭
hē	píjiǔ,		chī	fàn

To, for

The preposition 给 **gěi** (to, for) is located before the main verb in a sentence and is usually followed by a place or a person.

Practice these sentences with 给 **gěi**:

Subject	**gěi** + Place or person	Verb	Object
我	给她	买	电话卡。
Wǒ	gěi tā	mǎi	diànhuàkǎ.

I am buying a phone card for her.

您	给商店	打	电话
nín	gěi shāngdiàn	dǎ	diànhuà
她	给美国	回	电话
tā	gěi Měiguó	huí	diànhuà
我	给你	买	咖啡
wǒ	gěi nǐ	mǎi	kāfēi
她	给你	炒	鸡蛋
tā	gěi nǐ	chǎo	jīdàn

Too much

太 **tài** … 了 **le** (too, excessively, extremely …) is a frame with an adjective put in between 太 **tài** and 了 **le** to express a certain feeling.

Tài	*Adj*	*le*
太	贵	了。
Tài	guì	le.

It is too expensive.

▶

133

Practice making new sentences with this pattern using the adjectives provided.

好
hǎo

多
duō

少
shǎo

客气
kèqi

Possessive with 的 de

Practice using the possessive formed by a personal pronoun or noun followed by 的 **de**:

Subject	*Verb*	*Object*
这	是	您的房间。
Zhè	shì	nínde fángjiān.

This is your room.

我的电话号
wǒde diànhuàhào

您的电话卡
nínde diànhuàkǎ

宾馆的电话
bīnguǎn de diànhuà

你的八百三十块人民币
nǐde bā bǎi sānshí kuài Rénmínbì

我的护照
wǒde hùzhào (passport)

在 zài (be in/at)

她不在 **Tā bú zài.** (She is not here/there.) is a standard expression in which 在 **zài** is used as a verb and no place word follows it.

Question			Answer
Subject	zài	ma	Negative/Affirmative answer
马小姐	在	吗?	不在。/ 在。
Mǎ Xiǎojie	zài	ma?	Búzài. / Zài.
Is Miss Ma in?			(No, she is) not in. / (Yes, she is) in.

Practice this pattern using the subjects below:

王老师
Wáng Lǎoshī
(teacher)

黄经理
Huáng Jīnglǐ
(manager)

主任
zhǔrèn (office
director)

校长
xiàozhǎng
(school principal)

翻译
fānyì (translator)

To look for

找 **zhǎo** (to look for) is frequently used to say *I want to talk to … (over the phone) I want to see …* (when on a visit). Practice this very useful pattern.

Question			Answer		
Subj.	*Verb*	*Int*	*Subj.*	*Verb*	*Object*
您	找	谁？	我	找	马 小姐。
Nín	zhǎo	shéi?	Wǒ	zhǎo	Mǎ xiǎojie.
Who are you looking for?			*I am looking for Miss Ma.*		
			我		黄小姐
			wǒ		Huáng xiǎojie
			他		美国人
			tā		Měiguórén
			外国人		翻译
			wàiguórén		fānyì (translator)
			她经		理
			tā		jīnglǐ (manager)
			我		王老师
			wǒ		Wáng lǎoshī (Teacher Wang)

What's your surname?

When you meet a Chinese person the first time, use the polite way to ask his/her surname: 您贵姓? **Nín guì xìng?** *What's your surname?*.

The reply will be: 我姓 **Wǒ xìng** … *My surname is …*

Question			Answer		
Qǐng wèn	Subj.	Int	Subj.	**xìng**	Surname
请问,	您	贵姓?	我	姓	商。
Qǐng wèn	nín	guì xìng?	Wǒ	xìng	Shāng.
May I ask your surname?			*My surname is Shāng.*		

Practice asking and answering with this pattern using the following surnames:

Question			Answer		
Qǐng wèn	Subj.	Int	Subj.	**xìng**	Surname
					钱 Qián
					张 Zhāng
					马 Mǎ
					江 Jiāng
					王 Wáng

When asking for a full name say: 您叫什么? **Nín jiào shénme?** *What's your full name?* The answer will be: 我叫 **Wǒ jiào** …

Question				Answer		
Qǐng wèn	Subj.	**jiào**	Int.	Subj.	**jiào**	Full name
请问,	您	叫	什么?	我	叫	商美英。
Qǐng wèn	nín	jiào	shénme?	Wǒ	jiào	Shāng Měiyīng.
May I ask your name?				*I am called Shāng Měiyīng.*		

▶

Practice asking and answering with this pattern
using the question subjects, answer subjects, and names
provided:

Question Subj.	Answer Subj.	Full name
你	我	王民
nǐ	wǒ	Wáng Mín
他	他	张丁
tā	tā	Zhāng Dīng
她	她	李美
tā	tā	Lǐ Měi
那个人	那个人	吴用
nà ge rén	nà ge rén	Wú Yòng

Pronunciation Note
How to pronounce the initial "r"

When you say "r" in English, your lips are rounded. For
example: "read," "right." But when you say "r" in Chinese,
your lips should be close together and flat or spread. Your
tongue is rolled upwards with the tip near the base of the
upper teeth. You will feel the air vibrating around your
tongue. Your lower jaw should be thrust slightly forward.

Pinyin	Chinese	English
rè	热	hot
rén	人	people
Rìběn	日本	Japan

Pronunciation Practice

🔊 Read the following words aloud. Pay careful attention to the initial "r."

Pinyin	Chinese	English
1) ràng	让	to allow, to let, to yield
2) rè	热	hot
3) rèshuǐ	热水	hot water
4) rén	人	people
5) réngjiù	仍旧	still
6) suīrán	虽然	although
7) rènao	热闹	bustling
8) rénkǒu	人口	population
9) dǎrǎo	打扰	to disturb
10) wūrǎn	污染	pollution

🔊 Read the following words aloud. These words can help you to practice your pronunciation while learning some job titles that are used every day in China.

a. Service

1) xiǎojie 小姐 waitress, female attendant
2) fúwùyuán 服务员 server
3) shīfu 师傅 ("master") waiter, driver, chef
4) chúshī 厨师 chef, cook
5) yíngyèyuán 营业员 service employee

▶

6) shòuhuòyuán 售货员 store salesperson

7) lǐfàshī 理发师 barber

8) ménwèi 门卫 / kānménde 看门的 doorman

9) sījī 司机 driver

10) shòupiàoyuán 售票员 conductor, ticket clerk

b. Education

1) yuànzhǎng 院长 (dean)

2) xiàozhǎng 校长 (president, headmaster/
   headmistress)

3) jiàoshòu 教授 (professor)

4) lǎoshī 老师 (teacher)

5) jiàoshī 教师 (teacher)

6) xuésheng 学生 (student)

7) dàxuésheng 大学生 (college student)

8) jiāzhǎng 家长 (parents)

9) zhōngxuésheng 中学生 (secondary school
   student)

10) kēxuéjiā 科学家 (scientist)

11) xiǎoxuésheng 小学生 (elementary school
   student)

Sign for an IP public phone.
Can you recognize any of the characters?

Phone Calls: Part C

🔘 Listen to the CD and fill in the blanks with what you hear in Pinyin.

1)_____ 2)_____ 3)_____

4)_____ 5)_____ 6)_____

7)_____ 8)_____ 9)_____

10)_____ 11)_____ 12)_____

13)_____ 14)_____ 15)_____

🔘 Read and listen to the dialogue, then answer the questions below.

A: Foreigner 外国人 ***wàiguórén;***

B: Hotel attendant 服务员 ***fúwùyuán***

A: 请问，给美国打电话多少钱一分钟？

B: 给美国打电话三块五一分钟。

A: 给日本打电话多少钱一分钟？

B: 给日本打电话两块钱一分钟。

A: 用电话卡是不是便宜一点儿？

B: 是，用电话卡便宜。

A: 好. 谢谢。

B: 不谢。

Questions:

1. What is the rate for a call to the United States? _____

_____

2. What is the rate for a call to Japan? _____

_____

_____

3. What is the cheaper way to call? _____

_____

🔘   Listen to the words on the CD and write them below in Pinyin.

1) _____

2) _____

3) _____

4) _____

5) _____

6) _____

7) _____

8) _____

9) _____

10) _____

Fill in each blank with the appropriate measure word:

张	个	杯	瓶	块
zhāng	gè	bēi	píng	kuài

1) 我买一 _____ IP卡。

   Wǒ mǎi yì _____ kǎ.

2) 我换一百 _____ 钱。

   Wǒ huàn yìbǎi _____ qián.

3) 你要什么菜？我要一 _____ 鸡，三 _____ 馒头。

   Nǐ yào shénme cài? Wǒ yào yí _____ jī, sān _____ mántou.

Fill in each blank with the appropriate question word:

多少	哪儿	什么	谁	吗
duōshao	nǎr	shénme	shéi	ma

11)   一共 _____ 钱？

   Yígòng _____ qián?

2) 在 _____ 买电话卡？

   Zài _____ mǎi diànhuàkǎ?

3) 你们有 _____ 菜？

   Nǐmen yǒu _____ cài?

4) 请问，马丽莎在 _____ ？

   Qǐng wèn, Mǎ Lìshā zài _____ ?

You are staying in a hotel in China and want to call the United States. To prepare, translate these sentences into Chinese. Write your translations in Pinyin or characters.

1) How do I make a phone call to the United States?

_____

_____

2) What number should I dial first? _____

_____

_____

3) How much is it per minute to call the United States? __

_____

_____

_____

4) That's too expensive. Where can I buy a phone card?

_____

_____

Chinese Names

The order of Chinese names is different from that of English: the last name (family name or surname) comes first and the first name comes second. Chinese surnames usually have one character, for example: **Zhào** 赵, **Qián** 钱, **Sūn** 孙, **Lǐ** 李, **Zhōu** 周, **Wú** 吴, **Zhèng** 郑, and **Wáng** 王. There are, however, a few two-character surnames such as **Ōuyáng** 欧阳, **Sīmǎ** 司马 and **Shàngguān** 上官. Chinese first names usually have one or two characters.

In modern China, women do not take their husband's family name when they marry.

Public Phones

There are public phones on the street, at train stations, and in stores. Look for the sign 公用电话 **gōngyòng diànhuà** (public phone). There are coin or card-operated public phones, but most public phones have an attendant whom you pay after you make a call. You can also make long distance calls on public phones, for an additional fee.

At a Hotel: Part A

🔊 *Key Expressions*

你住哪个房间？ Nǐ zhù nǎ ge fángjiān?	Which room are you in?
我需要.... Wǒ xūyào....	I need....
请等一会儿。 Qǐng děng yí huìr.	Please wait a moment.
能换床单吗？ Néng huàn chuángdān ma?	Could you change my sheets?
...坏了。 ...huài le.	The...is broken.

🔊 *New Words 1* • 生词一

Characters	*Pinyin*	*English*
需要	xūyào	to need
条	tiáo	measure word for long, narrow things
毛巾	máojīn	towel

147

块	kuài	measure word for things in chunks or solid pieces
肥皂	féizào	soap
衣架	yījià	hanger
住	zhù	to live, to stay
哪个	nǎge	Which? Which one?
送	sòng	to send, to deliver
去	qù	to go; away (after a verb, indicating action directed away from the speaker)
卫生纸	wèishēngzhǐ	toilet paper
等	děng	to wait
一会儿	yí huìr	in a moment, shortly, for a little while

🔘 **Dialogue I · 对话一**

ROLES *A: Hotel guest* 房客 *fángkè;*
B: Hotel attendant 服务员 *fúwùyuán*

A: 小姐，我需要两条毛巾，一块肥皂，三个衣
架。
Xiǎojie, wǒ xūyào liǎng tiáo máojīn, yí kuài féizào,
sān ge yījià.

B: 你住哪个房间？
Nǐ zhù nǎ ge fángjiān?

A: 405 房间。
Sì líng wǔ fángjiān.

B: 我 给你送去。
Wǒ gěi nǐ sòng qù.

A: 我还要卫生纸。
Wǒ hái yào wèishēngzhǐ.

B: 我等一会儿 送去。
Wǒ děng yí huìr sòng qù.

A: 谢谢！
Xièxie!

B: 不客气。
Búkèqi.

Translation of Dialogue I

A: Miss, I need two towels, one bar of soap,
and three hangers.

B: Which room are you in?

A: Room 405.

B: I will send them to your room.

A: I also need toilet paper.

B: I will send it to you in a moment.

A: Thank you!

B: You are welcome.

How to read numbers:

A two-digit number is said in full, with the units (and not digit-by-digit). For example:

18	shíbā
22	èrshí èr
96	jiǔshí liù

A three-digit number may be said in full, with the units, or it may be said digit-by-digit:

405	sì bǎi líng wǔ *or* sì líng wǔ
713	qī bǎi yīshísān *or* qī yī sān

Four-digit numbers and above are usually said digit-by-digit, except that large round numbers may be also said in full, with the units:

17,924	yí wàn qī qiān jiǔ bǎi èrshísì
2002	èr líng líng èr
2,000	èr líng líng líng *or* liǎng qiān

给 **gěi** is a preposition meaning *to* or *for*. It is used when handing or transferring something to a person or when doing something on behalf of or for the benefit of a person. For example:

我 给 你 送 去。   I will send it over for you.
Wǒ gěi nǐ sòng qù.

This is different from the use of 给 **gěi** as a verb, meaning *to give*.

When 送 **sòng** means *to send, to deliver*, the person who does the action of sending must physically carry the object to a certain place. The distance of delivery can be either long or short. Notice, however, that when someone sends a letter through the mail, the verb *send* is 寄 **jì**, not 送 **sòng**.

🔵 New Words II · 生词二

Characters	Pinyin	English
能	néng	can; be able to
打扫	dǎsǎo	to clean, to sweep
你的	nǐde	yours
再来	zài lái	come again, come back
现在	xiànzài	now, present (time word: always placed before the verb in a sentence.)
可以	kěyǐ	may, can; may be permitted to
床单	chuángdān	bed sheets

床	chuáng	bed
厕所	cèsuǒ	bathroom, toilet
坏	huài	bad, broken, to become spoiled
坏了	huài le	to be out of order, to become spoiled
灯	dēng	light, lamp
修	xiū	to repair, to fix

🔊 Dialogue II · 对话二

ROLES A: *Hotel guest* 房客 *fángkè;*
B: *Hotel attendant* 服务员 *fúwùyuán*

A: 谁？请等一会儿。
Shéi? Qǐng děng yí huìr.

B: 能打扫你的房间 吗？
Néng dǎsǎo nǐde fángjiān ma?

A: 请等 一会儿再来。
Qǐng děng yí huìr zài lái.

* * *

A: 小姐,现在可以打扫我的房间了。请换床单。
Xiǎojie, xiànzài kěyǐ dǎsǎo wǒde fángjiān le. Qǐng
huàn chuángdān.

B: 好。
Hǎo.

A: 我的厕所 坏了，灯也 坏 了。
Wǒde cèsuǒ huài le, dēng yě huài le.

B: 一会儿给你修。
Yí huìr gěi nǐ xiū.

Translation of Dialogue II

A: Who is it? Just a minute, please.

B: May I clean your room?

A: Please come back later.

* * *

A: Miss, now you may clean my room. Please change the sheets.

B: OK.

A: The toilet doesn't work and the lamp is also broken.

B: We'll fix them for you shortly.

At a Hotel: Part B

Measure words 条 tiáo (long narrow piece) and 块 kuài (chunk)

条 **tiáo** is a measure word for things that are long and narrow in shape, such as:

两条毛巾 liǎng tiáo máojīn	two towels
一条鱼 yì tiáo yú	one fish
一条街 *or* 一 条路 yì tiáo jiē *or* yì tiáo lù	one street
一条裤子 yì tiáo kùzi	one pair of pants

块 **kuài** is a measure word for slices or chunks, such as:

一 块饼 yí kuài bǐng	a piece of fried bread
一块肉 yí kuài ròu	a piece of meat
一块糖 yí kuài táng	a piece of candy
一块肥皂 yí kuài féizào	a bar of soap

You have already learned that 块 **kuài** is used colloquially as a measure word for money (一块钱 **yí kuài qián**, *one yuán*). Originally, Chinese money was made of pieces of metal.

Simple directional complements 去 *qù (away)* / 来 *lái (towards)*

The simple directional complements 去 **qù** (away) and 来 **lái** (towards) often follow a verb to show the direction of the action relative to the speaker. Usually "main verb + 去 **qù**" indicates the action of the main verb is in the direction away from the speaker, and "main verb + 来 **lái**" indicates the action of the main verb is in the direction coming toward the speaker.

For example: 送去 **sòng qù** (sent to) is a phrase made up of two verbs in series. 送 **sòng** is the main verb and 去 **qù** is a secondary verb, a simple directional complement.

The adverb 一会儿 *yí huìr (in a while)*

等一会儿 **děng yí huìr** can mean either *to wait for a while* or else can be an expression meaning simply *in a while*. For example, 请等一会儿再来 **Qǐng děng yí huìr zài lái** means *Please come back in a while*.

Auxiliaries 能 *néng (can, be able to)* and 可以 *kěyǐ (can, may)*

In the dialogues in lesson 19, both 能 **néng** and 可以 **kěyǐ** are used to mean *permitted to*. They are both used before a verb:

能打扫你的房间吗？
Néng dǎsǎo nǐde fángjiān ma?

May I clean your room?

▶

你可以打扫我的房间了。   You may clean my room
Nǐ kěyǐ dǎsǎo wǒde fángjiān le. now.

In other instances 能 **néng** (can, be able to) refers to the
physical ability to do something, while 可以 **kěyǐ** (may, be
permitted to) refers to someone's having permission to do
something.

可以 打电话吗?   Can I use your phone to
Kěyǐ dǎ diànhuà ma?   make a phone call?

你不能打电话。电话坏了。 You can't make a phone
Nǐ bùnéng dǎ diànhuà.   call. the phone is broken.
Diànhuà huài le.

The negative form of both 能 **néng** and 可以 **kěyǐ** is
formed with 不 **bù**: 不能 **bùnéng** means *not able to* and
不可以 **bù kěyǐ** means *not permitted to*. Notice, however,
that 能 **néng** and 可以 **kěyǐ** are often used more ambigu-
ously in the dialogues in lesson 19. You see certain situations where 不能 打电话 **bùnéng dǎ diànhuà** and
不可以打电话 **bù kěyǐ dǎ diànhuà** are interchangeable.

The particle 了 le: a new situation

You have already learned that the aspect particle 了 **le**, following a verb, indicates that an action is complete.
了 **le** does not indicate past or present, but rather emphasizes that the action is finished.
  In this lesson the aspect particle 了 **le** at the end of a
sentence (or after an adjective) indicates a new or changed
situation. 现在可以打扫我的房间了 **Xiànzài kěyǐ dǎsǎo
wǒde fángjiān le** (You may clean my room now) literally

means *now is the time that now you are permitted to clean up my room* (but before this time you were not). 我的厕所坏了 **Wǒde cèsuǒ huài le** (My toilet is broken) means *now there is something wrong with my toilet* (but before it was working fine).

Measure words

Following the sentence structure below, ask for things using measure words.

Subj.	Verb	Number	Measure word	Object
我	需要	一	条	毛巾。
Wǒ	xūyào	yì	tiáo	máojīn.
I need a towel.				
		一	块	肥皂
		yí	kuài	féizào
		两	个	衣架
		liǎng	ge	yījià
		一	瓶	水
		yì	píng	shuǐ
		三	个	杯子
		sān	ge	bēizi
		一	卷	卫生纸
		yì	juǎn	wèishēngzhǐ
		一	条	床单
		yì	tiáo	chuángdān
		一	个	房间
		yí	ge	fángjiān
		一	个	灯
		yí	ge	dēng

Which room are you in?

你住哪个房间 **Nǐ zhù nǎ ge fángjiān?** (Which room are you in?) is a very common question that a hotel attendant will ask when you request something to be sent to your room.

Question				Answer		
Subj.	*Verb*	*Int.*	*Object*	*Subj.*	*Verb*	*Object*
你	住	哪个	房间?	我	住	405 号房间。
Nǐ	zhù	nǎ ge	fángjiān?	Wǒ	zhù	sì líng wǔ hào fángjiān.

Which room are you in?   *I am staying in room 405.*

Practice asking and answering questions with this pattern:

Question				Answer		
Subj.	*Verb*	*Int.*	*Object*	*Subj.*	*Verb*	*Object*
		多少号 duōshao hào				214
		多少号 duōshao hào	房间 fángjiān			321
		哪儿 nǎr				533
		哪个房间 nǎ ge fángjiān				这个房间 zhè ge fángjiān

To / from

Practice using the pattern of verb + simple complement, with 来 **lái** showing the action coming toward the speaker, and 去 **qù** showing the action going away from the speaker:

Subj.	Verb	Object	Subj.	Prep-phrase	Verb + *qù/lái*
我 Wǒ	要 yào	两个衣架。 liǎng ge yījià.	我 Wǒ	给你 gěi nǐ	送去 / 送来。 sòng qù / sòng lái.

I need two hangers.   *I will send them to you.*

	一条毛巾 yì tiáo máojīn	送来 sòng lái
	三块肥皂 sān kuài féizào	送去 sòng qù
	两个杯子 liǎng ge bēizi	送去 sòng qù
还要 hái yào	卫生纸 wèishēngzhǐ	送来 sòng lái
	电话卡 diànhuàkǎ	买去 mǎi qù
	人民币 Rénmínbì	换去 huàn qù

Soon

Practice using 一会儿 **yí huìr** to mean *to do something soon, in a while*:

Subject	Verb	*yí huìr*	Other elements
我	等	一会儿	送 去。
Wǒ	děng	yí huìr	sòng qu
I will send (it) to you soon.			
	去	一会儿	
	qù	yí huìr	
	看	一会儿	书
	kàn	yí huìr	shū
请	等	一会儿	打扫我的房间
Qǐng	děng	yí huìr	dǎsǎo wǒde fángjiān
	等	一会儿	再来
	děng	yí huìr	zài lái
	坐	一会儿	
	zuò	yí huìr	

To be able to

Practice asking and answering questions with 能 **néng** (can, be able to) followed by a verb.

Subject	Aux	Verb	Object
我	能不能	打扫	房间？
Wǒ	néng bùnéng	dǎsǎo	fángjiān?
May I clean the room?			

▶

Answer with 能 **néng** or 不能 **bùnéng**.

Subject	Aux	Verb	Object
		换 huàn	美元 Měiyuán
		修 xiū	灯 dēng
		买 mǎi	电话卡 diànhuàkǎ
		换 huàn	床单 chuángdān
		修 xiū	厕所 cèsuǒ

To be permitted

Practice asking and answering questions with 可以 **kěyǐ** (may, can, be permitted to) followed by a verb. Remember that the time word 现在 **xiànzài** must be placed either at the very beginning of a sentence or right after the subject and before the verb. It never comes at the end of a sentence.

"Now"	Subj.	Aux	Verb	Object	**ma**
现在	我	可以	打	电话	吗?
Xiànzài	wǒ	kěyǐ	dǎ	diànhuà	ma?

May I make phone calls now?

Answer with 可以 **kěyǐ** or 不可以 **bù kěyǐ**.

Practice this sentence structure using the verbs and objects provided:

▶

用	你的电话
yòng	nǐde diànhuà
去	银行
qù	yínghàng
吃	饭
chī	fàn
找	马小姐
zhǎo	Mǎ xiǎojie

To be broken

坏了 **huài le** (to have become out of order or broken) is a very useful expression for telling a hotel attendant that something is broken in your room and needs to be fixed.

Practice using this expression with the aspect particle 了 **le** following a verb to indicate a new or changed situation.

Topic	*Verb*	*Particle*
电话	坏	了。
Diànhuà	huài	le.
The telephone is broken.		
厕所		
cèsuǒ		
杯子		
bēizi		
灯		
dēng		
床		
chuáng		
菜 (Here 坏 **huài** means *bad, rotten*)		
cài		

Pronunciation Note
Vowels "ü" and "u"

The Chinese vowel "ü" has no equivalent in English. The lips are rounded when pronouncing both "ü" and "u", but the tongue has different positions. To pronounce "ü", place the tip of your tongue against the back of the lower teeth. But to pronounce "u", keep your tongue away from the teeth, with the tip not touching any part of your mouth. Practice this by first rounding your lips and keeping your tongue in the back of your mouth to pronounce "u". Then without changing the position of your lips, slowly move your tongue from the back to the front, so that it touches your teeth, and pronounce "ü". Pronounce "u" and "ü" several times, one after the other, to feel the difference in position. Notice that Pinyin omits the umlaut except after "l" and "n". Try these examples:

Pinyin	*Chinese*	*English*
1) lù [as in English "Luke"]	路	road
2) lǜ [no English equivalent]	绿	green
3) nú [no English equivalent]	奴	slave
4) nǚ [no English equivalent]	女	woman

Pronunciation Practice ◦

🔘 Read the following words aloud. Say the sounds carefully and listen for the difference between "ü" and "u".

"ü" (when following "y" or "j", the "ü" is written without the umlaut but still pronounced the same):

Pinyin	Characters	English
1) yú (yú)	鱼	fish
2) nǚ háizi (nǚ)	女孩子	girl
3) jūnduì (jūn)	军队	troops

"u" without umlaut, pronounced like the English "Luke":

Pinyin	Characters	English
4) rúguǒ	如果	if
5) nǔlì	努力	work hard
6) dùzi	肚子	stomach
7) zhǔnbèi	准备	to prepare

🔘 Read the following words aloud and pay special attention to the difference between "ü" and "u".

Pinyin	Characters	English
1) dìtú	地图	map
2) fùnǚ	妇女	women
3) lǚxíng	旅行	travel

▶

4) chūqù	出去	go out
5) cù	醋	vinegar
6) lúzi	炉子	stove

💿 Each entry below has an initial sound and a final sound that combine to form complete words. Read the initial and the final sound, then read the full word. Check your pronunciation on the audio.

Group A:		Group B:		Group C:		Group D:	
g	āi	y	áng	d	āi	zh	uāng
k	uài	w	ōng	t	uì	ch	í
h	uǎn	ü	ān	l	ún	sh	ùn
				n	uǎn	r	èn

💿 Read the following medical terms aloud.

1) shēntǐ	身体	body
2) bízi	鼻子	nose
3) bèi	背	back
4) ěrduo	耳朵	ear
5) dùzi	肚子	stomach
6) gēbo	胳膊	arm
7) liǎn	脸	face
8) yāo	腰	waist
9) shétou	舌头	tongue

10) shǒu	手	hand
11) tóu	头	head
12) tuǐ	腿	leg
13) yǎnjīng	眼睛	eye
14) zhǐjia	指甲	nail
15) yá	牙	teeth
16) zhèngzhuàng	症状	symptoms
17) fāshāo	发烧	fever
18) fālěng	发冷	chill
19) fāyán	发炎	infection
20) gǎnmào	感冒	cold
21) guòmǐn	过敏	allergy
22) késou	咳嗽	cough
23) hūxī	呼吸	breath
24) tóuyūn	头晕	dizzy
25) tù	吐	to throw up
26) lā dùzi	拉肚子	diarrhea
27) liúbítì	流鼻涕	runny nose
28) liúxuè	流血	bleeding
29) shāoshāng	烧伤	burn
30) téng	疼	hurt

🎧 Read the following hospital terms and doctor's instructions aloud.

1) yīyuàn	医院	hospital
2) yīwùshì	医务室	clinic
3) guàhàochù	挂号处	registration office
4) nèikē	内科	department of internal medicine
5) wàikē	外科	surgical department
6) yákē	牙科	department of dentistry
7) jízhěnshì	急诊室	emergency room
8) qǔyàochù/ yàofáng	取药处/ 药房	pharmacy
9) huàyànshì	化验室	laboratory
10) X-guāng shì	X光室	X-ray room
11) zhùshèshì	注射室	injection room
12) zhùyuànchù	住院处	admission office

Doctor's instructions:

13) Qǐng bǎ zuǐ zhāngkāi. 请把嘴张开.	Please open your mouth.
14) Qǐng bǎ shétou shēn chūlái. 请把舌头伸出来.	Please stick out your tongue.

15) Shēn hūxī.
深呼吸.

Take a deep breath.

16) Qǐng bǎ yīfu tuōdiào.
请把衣服脱掉.

Please take off
your clothes.

17) Tǎngxià.
躺下

Lie down.

18) Zhàn qǐlái.
站起来.

Stand up.

19) Qǐng bǎ xiùzi juǎn qǐlái.
请把袖子卷起来.

Please roll up your
sleeves.

At the Hotel: Part C

🔘 Listen to the compounds or phrases and write what you hear in Pinyin.

1)_____ lì   9) fǎ _____

2)_____ shì   10) mǎ _____

3)_____ xíng   11) fù _____

4)_____ lì   12) mì _____

5)_____ xùn   13) fèn _____

6)_____ shī   14) kǎo _____

7)_____ zi   15) bùjué _____

8)_____ zi

🔘 Read and listen to the dialogue, then answer the questions below.

First review these new vocabulary words.

zěnmeyàng 怎么样 (how)   búcuò 不错 (not bad)
liàng 亮 (bright)   gānjing 干净 (clean)
fúwùyuán 服务员 (attendant)

A: Male foreigner 男外宾 *nán wàibīn*;

B: Female foreigner 女外宾 *nǚ wàibīn*

A: 你住在几号房间？

B: 我住在302号房间？

A: 那个房间怎么样？

▶

B: 那个房间不错，很亮、很干净。你住在几号?

A: 我住306号。那个房间不太好.

B: 怎么不好?

A: 那个房间没有毛巾，床单也不太干净.

B: 你告诉服务员了吗?

A: 告诉了他们说给我送毛巾来，也给我换床单.

Indicate whether the following statements are true or false.

1) The room number of the female foreigner is 302.
   True (   )   *False* (   )

2) The male foreigner's room is in good condition.
   True (   )   *False* (   )

3) The female foreigner needs towels and clean sheets.
   True (   )   *False* (   )

4) The attendant will send towels and change the sheets.
   True (   )   *False* (   )

How many of the following things can you name in Chinese? Write the names in Pinyin in the blanks.

1) towels _____

2) soap _____

3) toilet paper _____

4) hanger _____

Exercise 3

Exercise 4

To prepare for your stay in a hotel in China, translate the following sentences into Chinese. Write the Chinese in Pinyin or characters.

1) I need one roll of toilet paper and three hangers. _____

_____

_____

2) My lamp is broken. _____

_____

_____

3) Who is it? Please come back later._____

_____

_____

4) Please clean my room now. Could you change my ___ sheets? _____

_____

_____

5) Please send one bar of soap and two towels to my room. I am staying in room 312. Thanks. _____

_____

_____

Categories of Hotels

The name of a hotel in Chinese usually reveals its rating. 宾馆 **bīnguǎn**, 饭店 **fàndiàn**, and 酒店 **jiǔdiàn** are usually four- or five-star hotels where most foreigners will stay. The staff in these hotels usually speaks English. 旅馆 **lǚguǎn** or 旅店 **lǚdiàn** are usually three-star (or below) hotels, and their staff usually do not speak English. 招待所 **zhāodàisuǒ** (guest houses or hostels) and 疗养院 **liáoyǎngyuàn** (health resorts) originally belonged to state-run companies or government agencies. Since the mid-1980s, with Economic Reform, most have become hotels. They usually are low-cost hotels, and only some of them let foreigners stay as guests.

Room Inspection at Checkout

Whenever you check out from a hotel in China, the front desk will ask you to wait while someone checks your room to verify that everything is in order. This is a routine part of checking out and happens to everyone.

22 Asking for Directions: Part A

 Key Expressions

请问，大门在哪儿？ Qǐng wèn, dàmén zài nǎr?	Excuse me, where is the gate?
英文系怎么走？ Yīngwénxì zěnme zǒu?	How can I get to the English Department?
一直走 yìzhí zǒu	go straight
左转 / 右转 zuǒ zhuǎn / yòu zhuǎn	turn left / turn right
附近有网吧吗？ Fùjìn yǒu wǎngbā ma?	Is there an Internet cafe nearby?

New Words 1 · 生词一

Characters	Pinyin	English
英文	Yīngwén	English language
系	xì	department (in a college)
英文系	Yīngwénxì	English Department

前	qián	front; forward, in front of; preceding
前边	qiánbian	in front, ahead
走	zǒu	to walk, to go, to leave
一直	yìzhí	straight, straight on, continuously
经过	jīngguò	to pass by, to pass through
大门	dàmén	main entrance
大	dà	big, large, major, old (when referring to age)
门	mén	entrance, door, gate
往	wǎng/wàng	to go; toward, in the direction of
右	yòu	right; right-hand
转	zhuǎn/zhùan	to turn, to change, to rotate
中文	Zhōngwén	Chinese language

中文系	Zhōngwénxì	Chinese Deparment
旁边	pángbian	side; beside, nearby
外教	wàijiào	foreign teacher (short form of 外国教师 wàiguó jiàoshī)
吧	ba	(used to make a mild imperative sentence, to imply agreement or a degree of certainty, to express unwilling-ness or hesitation)
教	jiāo/jiào	to teach
英语	Yīngyǔ	English language
附近	fùjìn	nearby; in the vicinity of, closely
网吧	wǎngbā	Internet cafe
右边	yòubian	right side
教学楼	jiàoxuélóu	classroom building
学	xué	to study, to learn; school, knowledge

| 图书馆 | túshūguǎn | library |
| 中间 | zhōngjiān | middle, center; in between |

 Dialogue I · 对话一

ROLES *A: Foreigner* 外国人 ***wàiguórén***;
B: Chinese person 中国人 ***Zhōngguórén***

A: 请问，英文系在 哪儿?
   Qǐng wèn, Yīngwénxì zài nǎr?

B: 在前边。
   Zài qiánbian.

A: 怎么走?
   Zěnme zǒu?

B: 一直走，经过大门，往右转，在中文系旁边。
   Yìzhí zǒu, jīngguò dàmén, wàng yòu zhuǎn, zài
   Zhōngwénxì pángbian.
   您是外教吧?
   Nín shì wàijiào ba?

A: 是，我在英文系教英语。请问，附近有网
   吧吗?
   Shì, wǒ zài Yīngwénxì jiāo Yīngyǔ. Qǐng wèn,
   fùjìn yǒu wǎngbā ma?

B: 有，在大门右边，教学楼和图书馆的中间。
   Yǒu, zài dàmén yòubian, jiàoxuélóu hé túshūguǎn
   de zhōngjiān.

177

Translation of Dialogue I

A: Excuse me, where is the English Department?

B: Up ahead.

A: How do I get there?

B: Go straight, pass the main gate and turn right. It is next to the Chinese Department. Are you a foreign teacher?

A: Yes, I teach English at the English Department. May I ask, is there an Internet cafe nearby?

B: Yes, there is one to the right of the main gate, between the classroom building and the library.

🔊 New Words II · 生词二

Characters	Pinyin	English
马路	mǎlù	road, street
对面	duìmiàn	on the opposite side, across the street
过	guò	to pass, to cross, to celebrate, to spend (time), to go through
远	yuǎn	far away, distant
左	zuǒ	left; left-hand
左边	zuǒbian	left side

书店	shūdiàn	bookstore
后	hòu	rear, back; behind, after
后边	hòubian	back, rear
大学	dàxué	university, college
办公室	bàngōngshì	office
外事处	wàishìchù	Foreign Affairs Office
商学院	shāngxuéyuàn	Business School
法学院	fǎxuéyuàn	Law School
留学生	liúxuéshēng	student studying abroad, foreign student
宿舍	sùshè	dorm
医院	yīyuàn	hospital
北京	Běijīng	Beijing
汽车站	qìchēzhàn	bus stop

🔊 Dialogue II · 对话二

ROLES *A: American* 美国人 ***Měiguórén;***
B: Chinese person 中国人 ***Zhōngguórén***

A: 请问，哪儿有厕所？
   Qǐng wèn, nǎr yǒu cèsuǒ?

B: 厕所在马路对面，过了马路往右走。
   Cèsuǒ zài mǎlù duìmiàn, guò le mǎlù wàng yòu
   zǒu.

A: 远吗？
   Yuǎn ma?

B: 不远。
   Bù yuǎn.

A: 怎么走？
   Zěnme zǒu?

B: 往前走，经过中国银行，银行的左边是书店，
   Wàng qián zǒu, jīngguò Zhōngguó Yínháng,
   yínháng de zuǒbian shì shūdiàn,

   书店的后边有一个厕所。
   shūdiàn de hòubian yǒu yí ge cèsuǒ.

Translation of Dialogue II

A: Excuse me, where is the restroom / public toilet?

B: It is on the other side of the street. Turn right after crossing the street.

A: Is it far?

B: It is not far.

A: How can I get there?

B: Walk straight ahead, and go past the Bank of China. To the left of the bank is a bookstore. The toilet is behind the bookstore.

Asking for Directions: Part B

在 zài (to be in/at)

在 **zài** (to be in/at) can be a preposition or a verb. 在 **zài** is a verb in the sentence 英文系在哪儿？ **Yīngwénxì zài nǎr?** (Where is the English Department?). In this sentence, 在 **zài** is followed by the interrogative pronoun 哪儿 **nǎr** (where). The answer is formed by replacing the interrogative pronoun 哪儿 **nǎr** with a noun of place, in this case 前边 **qiánbian** (front side). Here are some examples of 在 **zài** as a verb:

银行 在前边。 The bank is in the front.
Yínháng zài qiánbian.

马小姐在吗？ Is Miss Ma in?
Mǎ xiǎojie zài ma?

You can identify 在 **zài** as a preposition, rather than a verb, when there is a main verb in the sentence and when 在 **zài** is followed by a place word: 在 **zài** + place word + verb. Here are some examples of 在 **zài** as a preposition:

我 在 食堂 吃 饭。 I eat in the cafeteria.
Wǒ zài shítáng chīfàn.

他 在 银行 换 钱。 He exchanges money at the bank.
Tā zài yínháng huàn qián.

Sentences with subjects omitted

Adverbs (and adverbial phrases) are placed before the
verb in a sentence. Examples are:

怎么 zěnme (how)	*in*	怎么走？Zěnme zǒu? (How do I get there?)
一直 yìzhí (straight)	*in*	一直走 yìzhí zǒu (go straight)
往前 wàng qián (go forward)	*in*	往前走 wàng qián zǒu (walk forward)
左 zuǒ (left)	*in*	左转 zuǒ zhuǎn (turn left)

Notice that the Chinese word order is different from
English word order. In Chinese an adverb always precedes
the verb; in English it may follow a verb.

Left turn / Right turn

右转 **yòu zhuǎn** (turn right), 左转 **zuǒ zhuǎn** (turn left),
左走 **zuǒ zǒu** (walk towards the left) and 右走 **yòu zǒu**
(walk towards the right) are colloquial expressions that
omit the preposition 向 **xiàng** (towards) or 往 **wàng** (to,
towards).
The full form of 右转 **yòu zhuǎn** (turn right) is 向右
转 **xiàng yòu zhuǎn** or 往右转 **wàng yòu zhuǎn** (turn
towards the right); 左 **zuǒ** and 右 **yòu** are position words.
向右 **xiàng yòu** and 往右 **wàng yòu** are prepositional
phrases modifying the verb 转 **zhuǎn** (to turn).

在 zài, 有 yǒu and 是 shì (is, are)

Three verbs are used to describe a location:
a.   在 **zài** (to be in, to be at)
b.   是 **shì** (is, are)
c.   有 **yǒu** (there is/are)

a. To use 在 **zài** to tell the location of a place:

[TARGET PLACE] 在 **zài** [LOCATION]

The target place is the place someone is looking for, such as 英文系 **Yīngwénxì** (Department of English). The location is new information for the listener, and tells where the target place is.

With the verb 在 **zài**, the target place must come first, as the subject of the sentence. Then comes the verb 在 **zài**, followed by the location:

厕所在马路对面。 Cèsuǒ zài mǎlù duìmiàn.	The toilet is on the other side of the street.
教学楼在 英文系右边。 Jiàoxuélóu zài Yīngwénxì yòubian.	The classroom building is to the right of the English Department.

b. You can also use the verb 是 **shì** (is/are) to tell the location of a place.

[LOCATION] 是 **shì** [TARGET PLACE]

With the verb 是 **shì**, the location must come first as the subject of the sentence. Then comes the verb 是 **shì**, followed by the target place:

银 行的 左边是书 店。 Yínháng de zuǒbian shì shūdiàn.	On the left side of the bank is the bookstore.

马路 的 对面是厕所。   Across the street is the toilet.
Mǎlù de duìmiàn shì cèsuǒ.

---

c. The third choice is to use 有 **yǒu** (to exist, there is/are) to give information about the location of a place.

[LOCATION] 有**yǒu** (一个**yí ge**) + [TARGET PLACE]

The sentence pattern containing the verb 有 **yǒu** is the same as the pattern containing 是 **shì**, except that the target place usually is an indefinite noun preceded by the measure word 一个 **yí ge** (one, a).

大 门 旁边 有 一 个 网吧。   There is an Internet cafe
Dàmén pángbian yǒu yí ge   next to the main gate.
wǎngbā.

马路 对面 有 一 个 厕所。   There is a toilet on the
Mǎlù duìmiàn yǒu yí ge   other side of the street.
cèsuǒ.

A street intersection in Beijing

Asking locations with 在 *zài*

To ask for the location of a place with the phrase *Excuse me, where is ...?*, use the following pattern, with 在 **zài** (to be in/at) used as a verb:

请问 **Qǐng wèn** + location of a place + 在哪儿 **zài nǎr?**

The pattern for the answer is:

Target place	*Verb*	*Location*
英文系	在	前边。
Yīngwénxì	zài	qiánbian.

The English Department is straight ahead.

Practice asking and answering questions about the location of a place using the target places and locations provided:

外事处	大门旁边
wàishìchù	dàmén pángbian
网吧	马路对面
wǎngbā	mǎlù duìmiàn
教学楼	那边
jiàoxuélóu	nàbian
大门	左边
dàmén	zuǒbian
中文系	商学院后边
Zhōngwénxì	shāngxuéyuàn hòubian
法学院	英文系旁边
Fǎxuéyuàn	Yīngwénxì pángbian

Asking for directions

A frequently used pattern for asking directions is:

请问 **Qǐng wèn** + target place + 怎么走 **zěnme zǒu**?
Excuse me, how do I get to ...?

The pattern for answering this question is:

往 **Wàng** + direction + verb

Practice asking for directions using the words for target place, below. Notice that the verb comes at the end of the sentence, after the adverb (and adverbial phrase) that modifies it.

Question	*Answer*
请问, 网吧 怎么 走?	往 前走。
Qǐng wèn, wǎngbā zěnme zǒu?	Wàng qián zǒu.
How can I get to the Internet cafe?	*Go straight ahead.*

北京宾馆
Beijing Bīnguǎn

银行
yínháng

汽车站
qìchēzhàn

医院
yīyuàn

书店
shūdiàn

Giving directions

Practice giving directions with 转 **zhuǎn** (to turn) and
a direction word, which comes before 转 **zhuǎn**. Notice
that this is the opposite of English word order (turn left,
turn right, turn back).

Direction	*Turn*
左	转。
Zuǒ	zhuǎn.

Turn left.

左	右。
Zuǒ	yòu

Turn right.

左	后。
Zuǒ	hòu

Turn back

Practice adding 往 **wàng** (to, toward, in the direction of)
to this phrase.

Toward	*Direction*	*Turn*
往	左	转。
Wàng	zuǒ	zhuǎn.

Turn (towards the) left.

	右	
	yòu	
	后	
	hòu	
	北	
	běi	

Toward	Direction	Turn
南		
nán		
东		
dōng		
西		
xī		

Directions with 在 zài

Practice using 在 **zài** (be in/at) as a verb to tell directions.

The target place (the place someone is looking for) comes first, as the subject of the sentence. Then comes the verb 在 **zài**, followed by the location.

图书馆	在	前边。
Túshūguǎn	zài	qiánbian.

The English Department is straight ahead.

Practice forming sentences in this structure, using the following locations and target places.

Location	Target Place
宾馆	马路对面
bīnguǎn	mǎlù duìmiàn
中国银行	左边
Zhōngguó Yínháng	zuǒbian

Location	*Target Place*
厕所 cèsuǒ	大门 右边 dàmén yòubian
医院 yīyuàn	那边 nàbian
网吧 wǎngbā	商店旁边 shāngdiàn pángbian
电话 diànhuà	教学楼旁边 jiàoxuélóu pángbian
食堂 shítáng	后边 hòubian
汽车站 qìchēzhàn	左边 zuǒbian
医院 yīyuàn	宾馆右边 bīnguǎn yòubian

Directions with 是 shì

When the verb 是 **shì** (is/are) is used to tell the location of a place, the location comes first, as the subject of the sentence. Then comes the verb 是 **shì**, followed by the target place.

银行的左边	是	书店。
Yínháng de	shì	shūdiàn.

On the left side of the bank is the bookstore.

Practice forming sentences in this structure, using the following locations and target places.

▶

Location	*Target Place*
书店的旁边 shūdiàn de pángbian	商店 shāngdiàn
那边 nàbian	宾馆 bīnguǎn
教学楼的前边 jiàoxuélóu de qiánbian	食堂 shítáng
商店的后边 shāngdiàn de hòubian	邮局 yóujú
饭馆的右边 fànguǎn de yòubian	银行 yínháng
大门的左边 dàmén de zuǒbian	网吧 wǎngbā
马路的对面 mǎlù de duìmiàn	厕所 cèsuǒ

Directions with 有 *yǒu*

Practice using the verb 有 **yǒu** (there is/are) to tell the location of a place.

The sentence pattern with 有 **yǒu** is the same as with 是 **shì**, but the target place usually is an indefinite noun preceded by the measure word 一个 **yí ge** (one, a).

教学楼 的 旁边　　　有　　一个　　　书店。
Jiàoxuélóu de pángbian　yǒu　yí ge　　shūdiàn.
Next to the classroom building is a bookstore.

Practice forming sentences in this structure, using the words the following locations and target places.

▶

Location	*Target Place*
前边 qiánbian	厕所 cèsuǒ
宾馆的旁边 bīnguǎn de pángbian	饭馆 fànguǎn
大门的右边 dàmén de yòubian	网吧 wǎngbā
银行的后边 yínháng de hòubian	邮局 yóujú
饭馆的对面 fànguǎn de duìmiàn	电话 diànhuà
法学院的旁边 Fǎxuéyuàn de pángbian	商学院 shāngxuéyuàn
那边 nàbian	医院 yīyuàn
马路对面 Mǎlù duìmiàn	中国银行 Zhōngguó Yínháng

Pronunciation Note: The final "i"

In Pinyin the letter "i" represents three different vowel sounds, depending on which initial it follows.

🔵 Following most initials, the pronunciation of "i" resembles the English sound "ee".

Pinyin	*Chinese*	*English*
1) yī	一	one

2) qī   七   seven
3) dìdi   弟弟   younger brother
4) chūnjié   春节   Spring Festival
5) jīng   京   capital
6) jī   机   machine

Notice that in Chinese "i" is never pronounced as the English long vowel "i" (as in "right").

🔘 When "i" follows the initials "z", "c", or "s", it is pronounced as just an extension of the "z", "c", or "s", while the tip of your tongue stays against the back of lower teeth, and with vibration of the vocal cords.

Pinyin   *Chinese*   *English*
1) zì   字   character, word
2) cí   词   word, term
3) sī   丝   silk

🔘 When "i" follows the initials "zh", "ch", "sh", or "r" it is pronounced something like "r" and as just an extension of the "zh", "ch", "sh", or "r" with vibration of the vocal cords. With "zhi", "chi", or "shi" the tip of your tongue pulls back slightly from the roof of your mouth, but with "ri" the tongue does not move.

Pinyin   *Chinese*   *English*
1) zhīdao   知道   to know
2) chīfàn   吃饭   to eat a meal
3) lǎoshī   老师   teacher
4) jiérì   节日   holiday

Pronunciation Practice

🔘 Say the following words or phrases aloud, paying particular attention to pronunciation of the vowel "i."

Pinyin	Characters	English
1) Yīngwénxì	英文系	English Department
2) zìzhìqū	自治区	autonomous region
3) zìxí	自习	study by self in scheduled time or free time
4) mínǐ	迷你	mini (miniskirt)
5) chídào	迟到	to be late, to arrive late
6) háizi	孩子	child
7) sīchóu	丝绸	silk
8) sìshēng	四声	four tones
9) Rìběn	日本	Japan
10) cíqì	瓷器	porcelain
11) zhīshi	知识	knowledge
12) chǐzi	尺子	ruler
13) shīzi	狮子	lion

🔘 Each entry below has an initial sound and a final sound that combine to form complete words. Read the initial sound and the final sound, then read the full word. Check your pronunciation on the audio.

Group A:	Group B:	Group C:	Group D:
b ēn	zh èi	j uān	z òng
p éng	ch āo	q ū	c èng
m ián	sh éi	x uē	s uì
f ǎng	r ǎng		

🔘 Practice Pinyin by reading the following terms aloud.

1) diànnǎo 电脑 computer

2) diàndēngpào 电灯泡 light bulb

3) chāzuò 插座 socket

4) diàndēng 电灯 light

5) diànchí 电池 battery

6) yī hào diànchí 一号电池 D size battery

7) èr hào diànchí 二号电池 C size battery

8) wǔ hào diànchí 五号电池 AA size battery

9) qī hào diànchí 七号电池 AAA size battery

10) shōuyīnjī 收音机 radio

11) shǒujī 手机 cell phone

12) hūjī 呼机 beeper

13) CD-pán CD-盘 / jīguāng chàngpán 激光唱盘
    compact disc

14) lùyīndài 录音带 cassette tape

15) lùyīnjī 录音机 tape recorder

16) lùxiàngjī 录象机 video recorder

24 Asking for Directions: Part C

Exercise 1

💿 Listen to the words and phrases on the CD, then write the correct Pinyin spelling with tone marks in the blanks below.

1) _____

2) _____

3) _____

4) _____

5) _____

6) _____

7) _____

8) _____

9) _____

10) _____

Exercise 2

💿 Read and listen to the dialogue, then answer the questions.

First review these new vocabulary words:

图书馆 túshūguǎn (library)   从 cóng (from)

就 jiù (just)   电影院 diànyǐngyuàn

对 duì (correct)   (movie theater)

▶

A: English person 英国人 **Yīngguórén**;

B: Chinese person 中国人 **Zhōngguórén**

A: 请问图书馆在哪儿？

B: 哪个图书馆？是大图书馆吗？

A: 是。我要去大图书馆。

B: 你从这儿一直走，左边有一个电影院，过了电影院，就是大图书馆。大图书馆在左边。

A: 我从这儿一直走，过了电影院，左边就是大图书馆，对吗？

B: 对。

A: 好。谢谢!

B: 不谢!

Questions:

1. What does the English person want?_____

_____

2. What is the English person looking for?_____

_____

3. On which side of the library is the movie theater? _____

_____

_____

Change the following sentences into questions using the word in the parenthesis.

Examples:

大门对面有网吧。   (在) → 网吧在大门 对面。
Dàmén duìmiàn yǒu   Zài   Wǎngbā zài Dàmén
wǎngbā.   duìmiàn.

1) 商店旁边是书店。   (有)
   Shāngdiàn pángbian   yǒu
   shì shūdiàn.

2) 英文系在教学楼   (是)
   旁边。   shì
   Yīngwénxì zài jiàoxué-
   lóu pángbian.

3) 银行旁边是邮局。   (在)
   Yínháng pángbian shì zài
   yóujú.

4) 食堂在七号楼旁边。   (是)
   Shítáng zài qīhàolóu shì
   pángbian.

5) 马路对面是中国   (有)
   银行。   yǒu
   Mǎlù duìmiàn shì
   Zhōngguó Yínháng.

6) 书店后面有一个   (在)
   厕所。
   Shūdiàn hòumiàn yǒu zài
   yí ge cèsuǒ.

To prepare for a trip to China, translate the following sentences into Chinese. Write the Chinese in Pinyin or characters.

1) Where is the bathroom? _____

2) Where is the English Department? It is behind the classroom building._____

_____

3) How can I get to the Bank of China? Go straight, and then turn left. _____

_____

4) Is there an Internet cafe around here? The Internet cafe is on the left side of the gate. _____

_____

_____

5) Is it far? How can I get there?_____

_____

6) Excuse me, where is the bookstore? First go straight, pass the Bank of China, and then turn left. _____

_____

7) Is the hospital across the street from the main gate?____

_____

8) The post office is not far. _____

_____

City Districts

Cities in China are divided into districts. When you want to find a place in a city, you first need to find out which district it is in so you will know its general area. 北京 **Běijīng** has fourteen districts, of which 西城 **Xīchéng**, 东城 **Dōngchén**, and 宣武 **Xuānwǔ** districts make up the downtown area. Most foreign embassies and company offices are in the 朝阳 **Cháoyáng** district. Most universities, including Beijing University, are located in the 海淀 **Hǎidiàn** district.

深圳 **Shēnzhèn** is divided into six districts: 罗湖 **Luóhú**, 福田 **Fútián**, 盐田 **Yántián**, 南山 **Nánshān**, 龙岗 **Lónggǎng** and 保安 **Bǎo'ān**. **Luóhú** district is the downtown area of the city.

Street Names and Directions

Street names in China often include the words *east*, *west*, *north*, or *south*. For example, 天安门西大街 **Tiānānmén Xīdàjiē** literally means *Tiānānmén West Boulevard*, which tells you that the boulevard is west of **Tiānānmén** Square. Those directional words with a street name can help you find your way more easily.

Telling Time: Part A

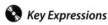 **Key Expressions**

现在几点？ Xiànzài jǐ diǎn?	What time is it now?
下午你有课吗？ Xiàwǔ nǐ yǒu kè ma?	Do you have class in the afternoon?
一起去…，好吗？ Yìqǐ qù…, hǎo ma?	Shall we go to…together?
…你常常做什么？ …nǐ chángcháng zuò shénme?	What do you often do in…?

New Words I · 生词一

Characters	Pinyin	English
几	jǐ	how many; a few, several
点	diǎn	o'clock; (decimal) point; to choose, to mark
几点	jǐ diǎn	What time?
差	chà	short of, wanting; to differ from
吧	bā	bar, cafe

吧	ba	(used to make a mild imperative, to imply agreement or a degree of certainty, to express unwillingness or hesitation)
上	shàng	first, upper; to go up, to get on
上午	shàngwǔ	morning, A.M.
午	wǔ	noon
半	bàn	half, partly
课	kè	class, course
上课	shàngkè	to go to class, to teach a class
汉语	Hànyǔ	Chinese language
下午	xiàwǔ	afternoon
下课	xiàkè	class is over; to dismiss class
刻	kè	quarter of an hour, 15 minutes
一刻	yí kè	one quarter of an hour, 15 minutes

三刻	sān kè	three quarters of an hour, 45 minutes
以后	yǐhòu	after; later on, afterwards;
一起	yìqǐ	together
好吗	hǎo ma	Is it OK? Shall we?
好吧	hǎo ba	OK, all right
见	jiàn	to meet, to see, to call on

🎵 **Dialogue I · 对话一**

ROLES *A: Chinese person* 中国人 ***Zhōngguórén***;
B: French person 法国人 ***Fǎguórén***

A: 现在几点？
    Xiànzài jǐ diǎn?

B: 现在差十分八点。
    Xiànzài chà shí fēn bā diǎn.

A: 我上午八点半要上汉语课。
    Wǒ shàngwǔ bā diǎn bàn yào shàng Hànyǔkè.

B: 下午你有课吗？
    Xiàwǔ nǐ yǒu kè ma?

A: 我下午有英语课。
    Wǒ xiàwǔ yǒu Yīngyǔkè.

▶

203

B: 你几点下课？
    Nǐ jǐ diǎn xiàkè?

A: 四点一刻。
    Sì diǎn yí kè.

B: 下课以后我们一起去网吧，好吗？
    Xiàkè yǐhòu wǒmen yìqǐ qù wǎngbā, hǎo ma?

A: 好吧，几点见？
    Hǎo ba, jǐ diǎn jiàn?

B: 五点五分我去找你。
    Wǔ diǎn wǔ fēn wǒ qù zhǎo nǐ.

Translation of Dialogue I

A: What time is it now?

B: Ten to eight.

A: I have Chinese class at 8:30 in the morning.

B: Do you have class in the afternoon?

A: I have English class in the afternoon.

B: When is your class over?

A: 4:15.

B: Shall we go to the Internet cafe together after your class?

A: OK. When shall we meet?

B: I will go to find you at 5:05.

Time word compounds
上午 **shàngwǔ** (morning), 中午 **zhōngwǔ** (noon), and
下午 **xiàwǔ** (afternoon) are compounds of 午 **wǔ** (midday) with 上 **shàng** (up), 中 **zhōng** (middle) and下 **xià**
(down). Their literal meanings are 上午 **shàngwǔ** *up to
midday*, 中午 **zhōngwǔ** *in the middle of midday*, and
下午 **xiàwǔ** *down from midday*. If you can remember that
上 **shàng** means *up*, 中 **zhōng** means *middle*, and下 **xià**
means *down*, it will be easy to remember 上午 **shàngwǔ**,
中午 **zhōngwǔ**, and 下午 **xiàwǔ**.

要 **yào** (to want; will)
You have already learned the use of the verb 要 **yào** as *to
want*:

我要一 张IP卡   I want to buy an IP phone card.
Wǒ yào yì zhāng IP kǎ.

But 要 **yào** can also be an auxiliary verb that comes before
the main verb and means *going to* or *will*, indicating that
an action or event will occur in the future:

我八点半要上汉语课。 I will go to Chinese class at 8:30.
Wǒ bā diǎn bàn yào
shàng Hànyǔkè.

上课 **shàngkè** and 课 **kè**
上课 **shàngkè** can mean *to go to class / to attend a class* as in:

我八点半要上课。   At 8:30 I will go to (attend or
Wǒ bā diǎn bàn   teach) class.
yào shàngkè.

but 上课 **shàngkè** can also mean *to begin a class* as in:

现在上课。   Class is beginning now.
Xiànzài shàngkè.

In both of those instances 课 **kè** means *class*, but when you say 汉语课 **Hànyǔkè** (Chinese language class), 课 **kè** means *course* or *subject*. 课 **kè** can also mean *lesson*, as in the chapter title 第九课 **dì jiǔ kè** (Lesson Nine).

去 **qù** (to go) can be directly followed by a noun of place:
去食堂   to go to the cafeteria
qù shítáng

去网吧   to go to the Internet cafe
qù wǎngbā

Notice that the noun following 去 **qù** must be a place. If you want to use a person's name or a pronoun after 去 **qù**, you must add 这儿 **zhèr** or 那儿 **nàr** after the person's name or pronoun. For example:
去你那儿   go to your place
qù nǐ nàr

When 去 **qù** is followed by another verb, as in 去吃饭 **qù chīfàn**, it is like the English phrase *to go (to) eat*.

▶

As you have already learned, when another verb precedes 去 **qù**, the 去 **qù** is a simple directional complement indicating that the action of the preceding verb is directed away from the speaker or the listener. For example:

我现在上课去。
Wǒ xiànzài shàngkè qù.

I go to class now. ["I" am not already in class.] or [I, the speaker, am moving away from the listener.]

🔘 **New Words II · 生词二**

Characters	Pinyin	English
早上	zǎoshang	morning
起床	qǐchuáng	to get up
洗澡	xǐzǎo	to take a shower, to take a bath
早饭	zǎofàn	breakfast
上班	shàngbān	to go to work, to go to the office
中午	zhōngwǔ	noon
午饭	wǔfàn	lunch
下班	xiàbān	to get out of work, to go off duty
晚上	wǎnshang	evening, night
常常	chángcháng	often

做	zuò	to do
跟	gēn	with
朋友	péngyou	friend
睡觉	shuìjiào	to go to bed, to sleep
有时候	yǒu shíhòu	sometimes, at times
以前	yǐqián	prior to, ago, before
晚饭	wǎnfàn	dinner
休息	xiūxi	to rest
睡午觉	shuì wǔjiào	to take a noon-time nap

🔊 **Dialogue II · 对话二**

ROLES *A: English person* 英国人 *Yīngguórén;*
B: German 德国人 *Déguórén*

A: 你早上几点起床？
Nǐ zǎoshang jǐ diǎn qǐchuáng?

B: 七点。起床以后我先洗澡，再去吃早饭。我九
点上班。
Qī diǎn. Qǐchuáng yǐhòu wǒ xiān xǐzǎo, zài qù chī
zǎofàn. Wǒ jiǔ diǎn shàngbān.

A: 你中午几点去食堂？
Nǐ zhōngwǔ jǐ diǎn qù shítáng?

B: 十二点我去吃午饭。
Shí'èr diǎn wǒ qù chī wǔfàn.

A: 你几点下班?
    Nǐ jǐdiǎn xiàbān?

B: 我五点下班。
    Wǒ wǔ diǎn xiàbān.

A: 晚上你常常做什么?
    Wǎnshang nǐ chángcháng zuò shénme?

B: 我常常跟朋友一起去饭馆儿吃饭。
    Wǒ chángcháng gēn péngyou yìqǐ qù fànguǎnr
    chīfàn.

A: 你几点睡觉?
    Nǐ jǐ diǎn shuìjiào?

B: 我有时候十一点睡觉，有时候十二点睡觉。
    Wǒ yǒushíhou shíyī diǎn shuìjiào, yǒushíhou
    shí'èr diǎn shuìjiào.

Translation of Dialogue II

A: What time do you get up in the morning?

B: At 7:00. After I get up, I shower, and then go for
    breakfast. I go to work at 9:00.

A: When do you go to the cafeteria at lunchtime?

B: I go to eat lunch at 12:00.

A: When do you get out of work?

B: I get off duty at 5:00.

A: What do you usually do in the evening?

B: I often go out to eat at a restaurant with friends.

A: When do you go to bed?

B: Sometimes I go to bed at 11:00, and sometimes at
    12:00.

Telling Time: Part B

Time words in a sentence

There are two kinds of time words in Chinese: words for specific times and words for time duration. In this lesson you will only learn words for specific times, such as *now*, *morning*, and *8:30*. Examples of time duration words are *one day* and *ten minutes*.

Position of time words in a sentence

Specific time words always come before the verb in a sentence. The time word may come at the very beginning of the sentence, or it may come after the subject but before the verb.

Time words at the beginning of a sentence:

现在几点？ Xiànzài jǐ diǎn?	What time is it now?
晚上你常常做什么？ Wǎnshang nǐ cháng- cháng zuò shénme?	What do you usually do in the evening?
五点五分 我去找你。 Wǔ diǎn wǔ fēn wǒ qù zhǎo nǐ.	I will go to your place at 5:05.

Time words after the subject but before the verb:

你早上几点起床？ Nǐ zǎoshang jǐ diǎn qǐchuáng?	What time do you get up in the morning?
我十一点睡觉。	I go to bed at 11:00.

Wǒ shíyī diǎn shuìjiào.

我下午有英语课。　　I have English class in the
Wǒ xiàwǔ yǒu Yīngyǔkè.　afternoon.

Note that when the time word is interrogative, it is located immediately before the verb:

你早上几点起床？　　What time do you get up in the
Nǐ zǎoshang jǐ diǎn　　morning?
qǐchuáng?

晚上你什么时候睡觉？　When do you go to bed in the
Wǎnshang nǐ shénme　　evening?
shíhòu shuìjiào?

Sequence of time words in a sentence

If there are two or more time words in a sentence, they appear in order from the broadest unit of time to smallest unit of time. For example, 11:30 in the morning will be 早上十一点半 **zǎoshang shíyī diǎn bàn** (literally: morning, 11 o'clock, half hour).

Specific time word + place + action

If you want to say that somebody is "doing something at some place at a certain time," the time words come before the place. For example: 我四点半在饭馆等你 **Wǒ sì diǎn bàn zài fànguǎnr děng nǐ** (literally: I, 4:30, at the restaurant, wait for you).

When telling time in Chinese, there is no need for a preposition such as 在 **zài** (at) before a time word. "I go to bed at 11:00" in Chinese is 我十一点睡觉 **Wǒ shíyī diǎn shuìjiào** (literally: I, 11:00, go to bed).

是 *shì in time expressions*

The verb 是 **shì** (to be) is not needed in time expressions, and it is usually omitted. If the verb is used, it appears between the topic and the number:

现在八点半。   It is 8:30 now.
Xiànzài bā diǎn bàn.

现在是八点半。   It is 8:30 now.
Xiànzài <u>shì</u> bā diǎn bàn.

A negative sentence must contain the negative form of 是 **shì**, which is 不是 **búshì** (to not be):

现在不是八点半。   It is not 8:30 now.
Xiànzài búshì bā diǎn bàn.

Verb-object words as intransitive verbs

起床 qǐchuáng (to get up)

洗澡 xǐzǎo (to take a shower, to take a bath)

吃饭 chīfàn (to eat a meal)

睡觉 shuìjiào (to go to bed, to sleep)

Each of the words above is formed by combining a verb with an object. This verb-object structure, which is common in Chinese, functions as a verb.

Before / after

The word order of 以前 **yǐqián** (before) or 以后 **yǐhòu** (after) in a Chinese sentence is the reverse of that in English, where *before* or *after* precedes a time or event. In Chinese these words follow a time or event word, so that the English *before 11:00* or *after class* becomes 11:00 以前 **yǐqián**, (*11:00, before*) or 下课以后 **xiàkè yǐhòu** (*class, after*). The placement of 以前 **yǐqián** (before) or 以后 **yǐhòu** (after) in a sentence is always between one time or event and another time or event.

我十一点以前睡觉。   I go to bed before 11:00.
Wǒ shíyī diǎn yǐqián
shuìjiào.

起床以后我先洗澡。   After I get up, I shower.
Qǐchuáng yǐhòu wǒ
xiān xǐzǎo.

Often / sometimes

The adverbs 常常 **chángcháng** (often) and 有时候 **yǒushíhòu** (sometimes) are treated as time words, and thus their placement in a sentence is the same as time words.

Asking what time it is now

To ask the time in Chinese, say:

现在	几点？	*What time is it now?*
Xiànzài	jǐdiǎn?	

The structure for answering this question is the subject, followed by the time:

现在　　　 七点五十分。

Xiànzài　　qī diǎn wǔshí fēn. *Now it is 7:50.*

Practice asking and telling the time in this sentence structure, using the times below.

> 2:00
>
> 4:15
>
> 7:30
>
> 5:05
>
> 6:45
>
> 9:10
>
> 8:55

Position of time words in a sentence

a. Time words at the beginning of a sentence.

When the time word is in the beginning of the sentence, the structure for asking questions is:

Time word	*Subj. + verb*	*Interrogative.*
下午	你 做	什么？
Xiàwǔ	nǐ zuò	shéme?

Literally, this means: *(In the) afternoon you do what?* ▶

214

To answer these questions, place the time word, which becomes the subject, at the beginning of the sentence. This is followed by the verb and the object. For example:

下午　　　我 上班。
Xiàwǔ　　　wǒ shàngbān.

Literally, this means: *(In the) afternoon, I go to work.*

Practice asking and answering questions in this sentence structure using the time words and verbs and objects below.

Time word	*Verb + object*
上午	上汉语课
shàngwǔ	shàng Hànyǔkè
晚上	给美国打电话
wǎnshang	gěi Měiguó dǎ diànhuà
下班以后	去换钱
xiàbān yǐhòu	qù huànqián

b. Time words between the subject and the verb.

When the time word is between the subject and verb, the structure is:

Subj.	*Time word*	*Verb + interrogative*
你	中午	做什么?
Nǐ	zhōngwǔ	zuò shéme?

Literally this means: *You (at) noon do what?*

To answer these questions, the structure is

Subj.	*Time word*	*Verb and object*
我	中午	休息。
Wǒ	zhōngwǔ	xiūxi.

I (at) noon rest.

▶

Practice asking and answering questions in this sentence structure using the time words and verbs and objects below.

Time word	*Verb + object*
下课以后	去网吧
xiàkè yǐhòu	qù wǎngbā
下午	上课
xiàwǔ	shàngkè
晚上	睡觉
wǎnshang	shuìjiào

c. The interrogative time phrase is located immediately before the verb.

In this structure, the subject comes at the beginning of the sentence, followed by the interrogative time word, followed by the verb and object. For example:

你	几点	起床？
Nǐ	jǐ diǎn	qǐchuáng?

Literally, this means: *You (at) what time get up?*

The structure for answering is the same as for asking: subject, followed by time word, followed by verb and object. For example:

我	六点	起床。
Wǒ	liù diǎn	qǐchuáng.

Literally, this means: *I (at) 6:00 get up.* ▶

Practice asking and answering questions in this sentence structure using the verbs + objects and the times below.

Verb + object	Time
睡觉 shuìjiào	10:30
吃早饭 chī zǎofàn	7:00
吃午饭 chī wǔfàn	12:00
上班 shàngbān	9:00
下课 xiàkè	3:45 P.M.

Specific time word + place + action

When you say that someone is doing something at some place at a certain time, the time words come before the place and the action. For example:

我	四点半	在饭馆	等你。
Wǒ	sì diǎn bàn	zài fànguǎnr	děng nǐ.
I	(at) 4:30	in the restaurant	wait.

Practice this sentence structure using the following time words, places and actions:

Time word	Place	Action
下午四点	在网吧	上网
xiàwǔ sì diǎn	zài wǎngbā	shàngwǎng

中午十二点	在食堂	吃饭
zhōngwǔ shí'èr diǎn	zài shítáng	chīfàn
晚上	在宾馆	上班
wǎnshang	zài bīnguǎn	shàngbān
上午	在银行	换钱
shàngwǔ	zài yínháng	huànqián

Before and after

Practice using 以前 **yǐqián** (before) and 以后 **yǐhòu** (after).

Time words	*yǐqián/yǐhòu*	*Subj.*	*Action*
八点	以前 / 以后	我	洗澡。
Bā diǎn	yǐqián / yǐhòu	wǒ	xǐzǎo.
I take a shower before/after 8:00.			
七点半			起床
qī diǎn bàn			qǐchuáng
下课			休息
xiàkè			xiūxi
中午			睡午觉
zhōngwǔ			shuì wǔjiào
下班			去商店
xiàbān			qù shāngdiàn
找马丽莎			一起去餐厅
zhǎo Mǎ Lìshā			yìqǐ qù cāntīng
三点			去网吧
sān diǎn			qù wǎngbā
换钱			买电话卡
huànqián			mǎi diànhuàkǎ

Often and sometimes

常常 **chángcháng** (often) and 有时候 **yǒushíhou** (sometimes) are also used as time words. In questions using these words, the subject comes first, followed by **chángcháng** then the verb + object and finally **ma**? For example:

你	常常	去饭馆	吗?
Nǐ	chángcháng	qù fànguǎnr	ma?

Do you often go out to restaurants?

To answer, start with the subject, followed by **yǒushíhòu,** followed by the verb (+ object). An answer to the question above could be:

我	有时候	去。
Wǒ	yǒushíhòu	qù.

I sometimes do.

Practice this sentence structure using the verb + objects below to ask the questions, and the verbs to answer.

Verb + object	*Verb*
换钱	换
huàn qián	huàn
去网吧	去
qù wǎngbā	qù
去商店	去
qù shāngdiàn	qù
买电话卡	买
mǎi diànhuà kǎ	mǎi
上汉语课	上
shàng Hànyǔkè	shàng

跟 gēn … 一起 yìqǐ …

The sentence structure for phrases with 跟 **gēn** …
一起 **yìqǐ** … (to do something with somebody) is:

Subj.	**gēn + person + yìqǐ**	*Verb*	*Object*
我	跟朋友一起	吃	饭。
Wǒ	gēn péngyou yìqǐ	chī	fàn.

I eat with a friend.

Practice forming sentences in this structure using the
people, verbs and objects below.

Person	*Verb*	*Object*
英国人	喝	咖啡
Yīngguórén	hē	kāfēi
王老师	去	换钱
Wáng lǎoshī	qù	huànqián
她	洗	衣服
tā	xǐ	yīfu
Liú小姐	去	商店
Liú xiǎojie	qù	shāngdiàn
马丽莎	上	课
Mǎ Lìshā	shàng	kè

Pronunciation Note

Differences between "j," "q," "x," and "zh," "ch," "sh"

Most English speakers need to pay special attention when learning Chinese to the differences in pronunciation between the initials "j," "q," "x," and "zh," "ch," "sh." You need to pronounce them accurately enough so a listener can distinguish between pairs such as

jiā 家 *home* and **xiā** 虾 *shrimp*, or

quán 全 *complete* and **chuán** 船 *boat*

The sounds of "j," "q," and "x" are produced with the tip of your tongue placed behind your lower front teeth and with the upper part of your tongue just behind your upper teeth. Your mouth should be stretched wide with your lips tight.

The sounds of "zh," "ch," and "sh" are produced with your tongue pulled somewhat back and with its tip just touching the roof of your mouth.

Notice that the initials "j," "q," and "x" only take "i" or "ü" (spelled "u") as finals or the head of finals. For example:

🔘 jī 鸡 chicken	jiā 家 home	juān 捐 to donate
qī 七 seven	qiā 掐 to pinch	quān 圈 circle
xī 西 west	xiā 虾 shrimp	xuān 宣 to declare

When you carefully listen to the sounds "j," "q," and "x," you will find there is always an "i" or "ü" included.

Pronunciation Practice

🔊 Read the following words aloud. Pay special attention to the differences between "j," "q," "x," and "zh," "ch," "sh." Check your pronunciation on the CD.

Pinyin	Chars.	English	Pinyin	Chars.	English
1) júzi	桔子	orange	zhúzi	竹子	bamboo
2) jūzi	锔子	cramp	zhūzi	珠子	bead
3) jiāng	姜	ginger	zhāng	张	to open
4) qiū	秋	autumn	chōu	抽	to take out (from in between)
5) qiáng	墙	wall	cháng	长	long
6) xùn	训	to train	shùn	顺	smooth
7) xuān	宣	announce	quān	圈	circle
8) zhuān	专	special	chuān	川	river
9) qúnzi	裙子	skirt	Xúnzǐ	荀子	surname of a Chinese philosopher
10) shàng	上	up	xiàng	向	toward

🔵 Each entry below has an initial sound and a final sound that combine to form complete words. Read the initial sound and the final sound, then read the full word. Check your pronunciation on the CD.

Group A:	Group B:	Group C:	Group D:
j iǔ	zh è	y (i) īng	z ài
q ián	ch ǎo	w (u) ǔ	c óng
x iǎo	sh āng	yu (ü) án	s ì

🔵 Practice Pinyin by reading the following words aloud.

1) jiājù 家具 furniture
2) shāfā 沙发 sofa
3) zhuōzi 桌子 table, desk
4) yǐzi 椅子 chair
5) shūguì 书柜 bookcase
6) cānzhuō 餐桌 dining table
7) diànshì 电视 TV
8) chuáng 床 bed
9) shuāngrénchuáng 双人床 double bed
10) chújù 橱具 kitchenware
11) guō 锅 pot, wok
12) bīngxiāng 冰箱 refrigerator

27

Telling Time: Part C

🔘 Listen to the words on the CD, and then write the correct Pinyin spelling with tone marks for each word in the blanks below.

1)_____   11)_____

2)_____   12)_____

3)_____   13)_____

4)_____   14)_____

5)_____   15)_____

6)_____   16)_____

7)_____   17)_____

8)_____   18)_____

9)_____   19)_____

10)_____   20)_____

🔘 Read and listen to the dialogue, and then answer the questions.

First review these new vocabulary words:

开门 kāimén (to open a door)   离 lí (from)

A: American 美国人 *Měiguórén*;

B: Chinese person 中国人 *Zhōngguórén*

A: 我要换一点儿钱。你知道银行几点钟开门吗？

B:　银行九点钟开门。

A:　现在几点了？

B:　现在八点。

A:　银行离这儿远吗？

B:　不远。就在书店旁边。

A:　好。谢谢。

B:　不客气。

Questions:

1. What time does this conversation take place? _____

_____

2. What time does the bank open? _____

_____

3. Why does the American want to go to the bank? _____

_____

4. Where is the bank located? _____

_____

Write the following times in Pinyin or Chinese characters:

   2:00 P.M. _____   4:10 P.M. _____

   6:15 P.M. _____   9:45 A.M. _____

10:05 A.M. _____ 11:00 A.M. _____

   8:30 A.M. _____   7:10 A.M. _____

12:00 P.M. _____   3:50 P.M. _____

   5:55 P.M. _____   1:00 P.M. _____

Exercise 3

Exercise 4

Fill in the blanks with the appropriate question word(s).

1) 你早上 _____ 起床？

   Nǐ zǎoshang _____ qǐchuáng?

2) 下课以后你做 _____ ?

   Xiàkè yǐhòu nǐ zuò _____ ?

3) 你跟 _____ 一起去商店？

   Nǐ gēn _____ yìqǐ qù shāngdiàn?

4) 晚上我去找你，_____ ?

   Wǎnshang wǒ qù zhǎo nǐ _____ ?

5) 电话卡 _____ 钱一张？

   Diànhuàkǎ _____ qián yì zhāng?

6) 厕所在 _____ ?

   Cèsuǒ zài _____ ?

7) 你下午上班 _____ ?

   Nǐ xiàwǔ shàngbān _____ ?

Exercise 5

To be able to communicate in Chinese, you will need to be able to talk about schedules. To practice, translate the following sentences into Chinese. Write the Chinese in Pinyin or characters.

1. What time is it now? It is five to ten. _____

_____

_____

▶

2. Shall we go to dinner together tonight?_____

_____

_____

3. What are you doing today? I am going to the Internet cafe after teaching English. _____

_____

_____

4. It is a quarter to four now. I will take a rest. _____

_____

_____

5. When do you go to bed everyday? I often go to bed at 11:00 P.M. _____

_____

_____

6. Sometimes I take a shower in the morning, sometimes in the evening. _____

_____

_____

7. I go to class in the morning, and go to work in the afternoon. _____

_____

_____

8. I get off work at 5:00 P.M. _____

_____

_____

Twelve-hour and 24-hour Time Systems

In China the 24-hour clock is used by the media, business and government, as well as for all official schedules, such as train and airplane times. In daily conversation, however, people usually use the 12-hour clock, and add *morning, afternoon* or *evening*: **shàngwǔ qī diǎn** (7:00 in the morning), **xiàwǔ sì diǎn** (4:00 in the afternoon), or **wǎnshàng jiǔ diǎn** (9:00 in the evening).

Operating Hours of Stores, Restaurants, and Government Agencies

Stores and restaurants are open seven days a week. Government agencies, including banks and offices, are open Monday through Friday. Daily working hours are 8:30 A.M.–5:30 P.M., with a one- or two-hour lunch break around noon.

Calendars: Part A

 Key Expressions

今天星期几？ Jīntiān xīngqījǐ?	What day of the week is it today?
周末我洗衣服。 Zhōumò wǒ xǐ yīfu.	I do laundry on the weekends.
八月十号是我的生日。 Bāyuè shí hào shì wǒde shēngrì.	August 10 is my birthday.
我今年二十岁。 Wǒ jīnnián èrshí suì.	I am twenty this year.

 New Words 1 · 生词一

Characters	Pinyin	English
今天	jīntiān	today
星期几	xīngqījǐ	What day of the week?
星期	xīngqī	week
星期二	xīngqī'èr	Tuesday
明天	míngtiān	tomorrow
星期三	xīngqīsān	Wednesday

每	měi	every, each
每天	měi tiān	every day
星期五	xīngqīwǔ	Friday
节	jié	section, segment, period (of a class); festival, holiday
钟头	zhōngtóu	hour
对	duì	right, correct
不对	búduì	incorrect, wrong
只有	zhǐyǒu	only; only if
星期一	xīngqīyī	Monday
星期四	xīngqīsì	Thursday
天	tiān	day
工作	gōngzuò	to work; work, job
外国	wàiguó	foreign country
公司	gōngsī	company, corporation, firm
做	zuò	to be, to act as

翻译	fānyì	translator, interpreter; to translate, to interpret
周末	zhōumò	weekend
星期六	xīngqīliù	Saturday
家	jiā	home, family
休息	xiūxi	to rest
洗	xǐ	to wash
衣服	yīfu	clothes, clothing
洗衣服	xǐ yīfu	to do laundry, to wash clothes
星期日	xīngqīrì	Sunday
看	kàn/kān	to watch, to see; to look after
电视	diànshì	television
可能	kěnéng	may, might; possible
电影	diànyǐng	movie

🔘 **Dialogue I · 对话一**

ROLES *A:* 周文 **Zhóu Wén**;
         B: 马明 **Mǎ Míng**

A.   今天星期几？
      Jīntiān xīngqījǐ?

B.   星期二。
      Xīngqī'èr.

A.   明天星期三。我有中文课。
      Míngtiān xīngqīsān. Wǒ yǒu Zhōngwénkè.

B.   你每天都有中文课吗？
      Nǐ měitiān dōu yǒu Zhōngwénkè ma?

A.   不，星期三和星期五下午我有中文课，学
      中文。
      Bù, xīngqīsān hé xīngqīwǔ xiàwǔ wǒ yǒu Zhōng-
      wénkè, xué Zhōngwén.

B.   你每天上几节中文课？
      Nǐ měitiān shàng jǐ jié Zhōngwénkè?

A.   两节。
      Liǎng jié.

B.   一节课是一个钟头，对不对？
      Yì jié kè shì yí ge zhōngtóu[6], duì búduì?

A.   不。一节课只有五十分钟。
      Bù. Yì jié kè zhǐyǒu wǔshí fēnzhōng.

B.   星期一，星期二和星期四你都没有课吗？
      Xīngqīyī, xīngqī'èr hé xīngqīsì nǐ dōu méiyǒu kè
      ma?

A.   这三天我工作，我在一个外国公司做翻译。
      Zhè sān tiān wǒ gōngzuò. Wǒ zài yí ge wàiguó
      gōngsī zuò fānyì.

▶

B. 这个周末你做什么？
Zhè ge zhōumò nǐ zuò shénme?

A. 星期六在家休息,洗衣服。星期日看电视，
也可能去看电影。
Xīngqīliù zài jiā xiūxi, xǐ yīfu. Xīngqīrì kàn diànshì, yě kěnéng qù kàn diànyǐng.

Translation of Dialogue I

A: What day is it today?

B: Tuesday.

A: Tomorrow is Wednesday. I have Chinese class.

B: Do you have Chinese class every day?

A: No, on Wednesday and Friday afternoons I have
Chinese class; I study Chinese.

B: How many Chinese classes do you have each day?

A: Two.

B: Each class is one hour, is that correct?

A: No. Each class is only fifty minutes.

B: You don't have classes on Monday, Tuesday and
Thursday, do you?

A: Those three days I work. I am a translator for a
foreign company.

B: What will you do this weekend?

A: I will rest and do laundry at home on Saturday. I
will watch TV on Sunday. I may go to a movie.

In the dialogue, 几 **jǐ** (which, what) is an interrogative used to ask for a date, time, or number:

几月 jǐyuè?	What month?
几号 jǐhào?	What date? What number?
几点 jǐdiǎn?	What time? What hour?
星期几 xīngqījǐ?	What day of the week?

When followed by a measure word, 几 **jǐ** is also used to ask the quantity of something. For example:

几个钟头 jǐ ge zhōngtóu?	How many hours?
几分钟 jǐ fēnzhōng?	How many minutes?
几天 jǐtiān?	How many days?
几年 jǐnián?	How many years?

中文 **Zhōngwén** (the Chinese language)

There are four ways to refer to the Chinese language. 中文 **Zhōngwén** originally referred to the written Chinese language but now generally also includes spoken Chinese. A more precise term for the Chinese language is 汉语 **Hànyǔ**, which covers both the spoken and the written Chinese. 中国话 **Zhōngguóhuà** is a colloquial term for spoken Chinese. 普通话 **Pǔtōnghuà** is the official name for Mandarin.

每天 **měi tiān** + **dōu** + verb

In Chinese, 每天 **měi tiān** means *every day*. 都 **dōu** (all) is placed before the verb and emphasizes doing the same thing every day.

学 **xué** (to study) as a transitive verb can be followed by
a noun, as in 学中文 **xué Zhōngwén** (to study Chinese)
and 学英文 **xué Yīngwén** (to study English). It can also
be followed by a verb, as in 学数数 **xué shǔ shù** (to learn
counting).

节 **jié** (section, length, segment) is a measure word for
class periods, train cars, and batteries. 一节课 **yì jié kè**
means *one class period*.

When counting hours, use the measure word 个 **ge** before
钟头 **zhōngtóu** (hour):

一个钟头 yí ge zhōngtóu   one hour

四个钟头 sì ge zhōngtóu   four hours

个 **ge** is also used with the more formal term
小时 **xiǎoshí** (hour): 一个小时 **yí ge xiǎoshí** (one hour).

分钟 **fēnzhōng** (minute) is used when counting minutes
(duration of time).

休息 **xiūxi** (to rest, to relax) is an intransitive verb and
thus cannot be followed by a noun, but it can be followed
by a word or phrase of time duration:

休息十分钟   to rest for ten minutes
xiūxi shí fēnzhōng

休息一会儿   to have a break (for a little
xiūxi yí huìr   while)

New Words II · 生词二

Characters	Pinyin	English
号	hào	date
几号	jǐhào	What date (of the month)? What number?
月	yuè	month
八月	bāyuè	August
生日	shēngrì	birthday
哪年	nǎnián	Which year?
年	nián	year
出生	chūshēng	to be born
生	shēng	to give birth to, to be born, to grow; life; raw
今年	jīnnián	this year
岁	suì	year of age, year old
多大	duōdà	How old?
四月	sìyuè	April
大	dà	old (when referring to age)

过	guò	to pass, to cross; to celebrate, to spend (time); to go through
过生日	guò shēngrì	to celebrate a birthday
明年	míngnián	next year
想	xiǎng	to want, to think
星期天	xīngqītiān	Sunday
昨天	zuótiān	yesterday
前天	qiántiān	the day before yester day
后天	hòutiān	the day after tomor row
上个	shàng ge	previous, first part of
上个星期	shàng ge xīngqī	last week
这个星期	zhè ge xīngqī	this week
下个	xià ge	next, second, latter
下个星期	xià ge xīngqī	next week

每个	měi ge	every, each
每个星期	měi ge xīngqī	every week, weekly
去年	qùnián	last year
上个月	shàng ge yuè	last month
这个月	zhè ge yuè	this month
下个月	xià ge yuè	next month

🔘 Dialogue II · 对话二

ROLES *A: Foreigner* 外国人 *wàiguórén;*
B: Chinese person 中国人 *Zhōngguórén*

A. 今天几号？
   Jīntiān jǐ hào?

B. 今天八月十号。
   Jīntiān bāyuè shí hào.

A. 明天八月十一号，是我的生日。
   Míngtiān bāyuè shíyī hào, shì wǒde shēngrì.

B. 你是哪年出生的？
   Nǐ shì nǎnián chūshēng de?

A. 我是一九八五年生的。我今年二十一岁了。
   你呢？你多大了？
   Wǒ shì yī jiǔ bā wǔ nián shēng de. Wǒ jīnnián
   èrshíyī suì le. Nǐ ne? Nǐ duō dà le?

B. 我今年三十九岁。
   Wǒ jīnnián sānshíjiǔ suì.

A. 你的生日是哪天？
   Nǐde shēngrì shì nǎ tiān?

B. 我的生日是四月六号。我是在美国过的生日。
   Wǒde shēngrì shì sìyuè liù hào. Wǒ shì zài Měiguó
   guò de shēngrì.
   明天我们在北京给你过生日。
   Míngtiān wǒmen zài Beijing gěi nǐ guò shēngrì.

A. 太好了！谢谢！
   Tài hǎo le! Xièxie!

B. 明年我也想在北京过生日。
   Míngnián wǒ yě xiǎng zài Běijīng guò shēngrì.

Translation of Dialogue II

A: What day is it today?

B: Today is August 10.

A: Tomorrow is August 11. It is my birthday.

B: Which year were you born?

A: I was born in 1985. I am twenty-one this year.
    How about you? How old are you?

B: I am thirty-nine this year.

A: Which day is your birthday?

B: My birthday is April 6. I celebrated my birthday
      in the United States. Tomorrow we will celebrate
      your birthday in Beijing.

A: That's great! Thank you.

B: I also want to celebrate my birthday in Beijing
      next year.

你多大了？ **Nǐ duō dà le?** (How old are you?) is a question for someone who is in the same generation as you. When asking people who are older than you, use the more polite 您 **nín** instead of 你 **nǐ**: 您多大年纪了？ **Nín duō dà niánjì le?**" (How old are you?). To ask the age of a child under ten, say: 你几岁了？ **Nǐ jǐ suì le?** (How old are you?). This is because **jǐ** 几 is usually used for numbers less than ten.

Calendars: Part B

The days of the week

Until recently, the Chinese counted days only in months, not weeks. Then, at the beginning of the twentieth century, the concept of *week* 星期 **xīngqī** was adopted from the West. There are no special names for the seven days of the week in Chinese. Instead, the days Monday through Saturday are simply stated as 星期 **xīngqī** followed by a number from one to six, and Sunday is stated as 星期 **xīngqī** followed by 日 **rì** or 天 **tiān**. The literal meaning of 星期 **xīngqī** is *star period*.

English Day of week	*Xīngqī + Number*
Monday	星期 xīngqī 一 yī
Tuesday	星期 xīngqī 二 èr
Wednesday	星期 xīngqī 三 sān
Thursday	星期 xīngqī 四 sì
Friday	星期 xīngqī 五 wǔ
Saturday	星期 xīngqī 六 liù
Sunday	星期 xīngqī 日 rì / 星期天 xīngqītiān

Time description

the day before yesterday	前天 qiántiān
yesterday	昨天 zuótiān
today	今天 jīntiān
tomorrow	明天 míngtiān

▶

the day after tomorrow	后天 hòutiān
last year	去年 qùnián
this year	今年 jīnnián
next year	明年 míngnián

Measure words in dates

You might have noticed 这三天 **zhè sān tiān** (these three days) and 这个周末 **zhè ge zhōumò** (this weekend) from the dialogue in lesson 28. When counting 天 **tiān** (days) or 年 **nián** (years), there is no need for a measure word. For example:

| 三天 sān tiān | three days |
| 两年 liǎng nián | two years |

But when counting 星期 **xīngqī** (weeks) or 月 **yuè** (months), the measure word 个 **ge** must be added before 星期 **xīngqī** and 月 **yuè**. For example:

| 三个星期 sān ge xīngqī | three weeks |
| 两个月 liǎng ge yuè | two months |

这个 **zhè ge** (this) indicates the current day, week, weekend, month, etc. Unlike English, a day in the current week can be modified by 这个 **zhè ge** regardless of whether that day is already past or is to come. 上个 **shàng ge** means *last*, 下个 **xià ge** means *next* and 每个 **měi ge** means *every*.

这个星期三 zhè ge xīngqīsān	this Wednesday
这个周末 zhè ge zhōumò	this weekend
下个周末 xià ge zhōumò	next weekend
上个星期 shàng ge xīngqī	last week

▶

下个星期 xià ge xīngqī   next week
每个星期 měi ge xīngqī   every week
上个月 shàng ge yuè   last month
下个月 xià ge yuè   next month
每个月 měi ge yuè   every month

Months

The names of the twelve months are stated by simply combining a number from one to twelve with 月 **yuè** (month).

English	Number	+	月 *yuè*
January	一 yí		月 yuè
February	二 èr		月 yuè
March	三 sān		月 yuè
April	四 sì		月 yuè
May	五 wǔ		月 yuè
June	六 liù		月 yuè
July	七 qī		月 yuè
August	八 bā		月 yuè
September	九 jiǔ		月 yuè
October	十 shí		月 yuè
November	十一 shíyī		月 yuè
December	十二 shíèr		月 yuè

The days of the month are stated by simply combining a number from one to thirty-one with 号 **hào** or 日 **rì** (day).

一号 yí hào, 二号 èr hào, 三号 sān hào…三十一号 sānshíyí hào

Sequence of year, month, date

If the month is given, it will come before the day, so *January 1* is 一月一号 **yíyuè yí hào**. Just as you've learned with regard to telling time, the sequence of time words is from the largest unit of time to the smallest unit of time. So for dates, the sequence is year, month, day of the month. For example:

2004年1月1号下午5点   5 P.M. on January 1, 2004
èr líng líng sì nián yí yuè
yí hào xiàwǔ wǔ diǎn

去年三月五号   March 5 of last year
qùnián sānyuè wǔ hǎo

是 **shì** (to be) usually is omitted when expressing time, although it is necessary in a negative sentence with 不是 **búshì** (to not be), for example:

今天星期一。   Today (is) Monday.
Jīntiān xīngqīyī.

他十九岁。   He (is) nineteen years old.
Tā shíjiǔ suì.

今天不是八月十号。   Today is not August 10.
Jīntiān búshì bāyuè shí
hào.

The sentence pattern "是 shì ... 的 de"

This sentence pattern is used for emphasizing the time, place, or manner of an action or event that occurred in the past. For example, the following way of asking someone's age places special emphasis on the specific year:

你是哪年出生的？ Nǐ shì nǎ nián chūshēng de?	What year were you born?
我是1981年生的。 Wǒ shì yī jiǔ bā yī nián shēng de.	I was born in 1981.

The next example emphasizes the manner of an action:

我是坐车去的。 Wǒ shì zuò chē qù de.	I went by bus.

If the verb indicating the action or event is a verb-object combination, 的 **de** can be either placed between the verb and the object or after the verb-object, with no difference in meaning. For example:

你是在哪儿换的钱？ Nǐ shì zài nǎr huàn de qián?	Where did you change your money?

or

你是在哪儿换钱的？ Nǐ shì zài nǎr huànqián de?	Where did you change your money?

How to say the year

A year is stated digit by digit, followed by the word
年 **nián** (year):

一九八一年 yī jiǔ bā yī nián	1981
二〇〇四年 èr líng líng sì nián	2004

What day is it?

To ask about days of the week in Chinese, begin the sentence with the subject, followed by the time word, followed by the interrogative, 几 **jǐ**.

今天　　星期　几?

| Jīntiān | xīngqī jǐ? | *What day of the week is it today?* |

To answer this question, simply use the same subject, followed by the time word.

今天　　星期一。

| Jīntiān | xīngqīyī. | *Today is Monday.* |

Practice the days of the week, as in the example, using the subjects and time words below.

Subject	*Time word*
明天	星期五
míngtiān	xīngqīwǔ
昨天	星期三
zuótiān	xīngqīsān
前天	星期二
qiántiān	xīngqīèr
后天 (the day after tomorrow)	星期四
hòutiān	xīngqīsì
六号	星期六
liù hào	xīngqīliù
十五号	星期日
shíwǔ hào	xīngqīrì
二十七号	星期天
èrshíqī hào	xīngqītiān

Measure words

When you talk about days (天 **tiān**) or years (年 **nián**), no measure word is needed. But when saying how many weeks and months, the measure word 个 **ge** is needed.

Practice saying how many days or years by saying the following numbers with 天 **tiān** or 年 **nián**.

Number	*tiān*	Number	*nián*
一	天	一	年
yì	tiān	yì	nián
one day		*one year*	
五		三	
两		四	
九		十	
三十一		十五	
二十		一百	
七十		六十	

Practice saying how many weeks or months by saying the following numbers with 星期 **xīngqī**, *week* or 月 **yuè**, *month*.

Number	*ge*	*week*	Number	*ge*	*month*
一	个	星期	一	个	月
yí	ge	xīngqī	yí	ge	yuè
one week			*one month*		
三			两		
六			五		
十			十二		
四			七		
八			九		

Asking someone's birthday

To ask someone's birthday, say:

你 的 生日 是 几月几号？
Nǐ de shēngrì shì jǐyuè jǐhào?   What day is your
                                   birthday?

To answer this question, start with the subject (my, his, etc.), followed by the verb, then the date, for example:

我的 生日 是 五月 七号。
Wǒde shēngrì shì wǔyuè qī hào.   My birthday is
                                   May 7.

Practice asking about and telling people's birthdays using the subjects and dates below.

Subject	*Date*
他	十月一号
tā	shíyuè yí hào
王小姐	八月六号
Wáng xiǎojie	bāyuè liù hào
你朋友	四月九号
nǐ péngyou	sìyuè jiǔ hào
中文老师	六月三十一号
Zhōngwén lǎoshī	liùyuè sānshíyī hào
英文老师	十二月十五号
Yīngwén lǎoshī	shí'èryuè shíwǔ hào

To ask someone what he does on a certain day, or at a certain time, use the following structure:

Time	*Subj.*	*Verb*	*Int.*
周末	你	做	什么？
Zhōumò	nǐ	zuò	shénme?

Literally, this means: *Weekend you do what?* or, *What do you do on the weekend?*

Your answer would simply be the subject (*I*) followed by the verb and object to describe your activities.

我	洗	衣服。
Wǒ	xǐ	yīfu.

I do laundry.

Practice asking and answering the question *What do you do on ...?* using the times, verbs and objects below.

Time	*Verb*	*Object*
星期三		中文课
xīngqīsān		shàng Zhōngwénkè
星期二上午	教	英语
xīngqī'èr shàngwǔ	jiāo	Yīngyǔ
星期日下午	休息	
xīngqīrì xiàwǔ		xiūxi
明天		去 商店
míngtiān		qù shāngdiàn
今天晚上	看	电视
jīntiān wǎnshang	kàn	diànshì
这个星期六	看	电影
zhè ge xīngqīliù	kàn	diànyǐng
星期四上午	去	换钱
xīngqīsì shàngwǔ	qù	huànqián
中午		睡 午觉
zhōngwǔ		shuì wǔjiào

Pronunciation Note

Accurate pronunciation of "u"

It is very common for English speakers to mispronounce 五 **wǔ** with the "u" not long enough. Remember that for "u" in Pinyin, the English equivalent sound is "oo." For example:

Pinyin	*Characters*	*English*
1) wǔ	五	five
2) wūzi	屋子	room
3) wǔshù	武术	martial arts
4) tǔdì	土地	land, earth
5) gǔdài	古代	ancient time
6) mǔqin	母亲	mother
7) dǔchē	堵车	traffic jam
8) dúyào	毒药	poison

Pronunciation Practice

🔊 Read the following words and phrases aloud, paying special attention to "u."

Pinyin	Characters	English
1) wūyún	乌云	black cloud
2) wūguī	乌龟	turtle
3) wūlóngchá	乌龙茶	Oolong tea
4) Wúxī	无锡	(city name)
5) wúhuāguǒ	无花果	fig
6) wúmíng	无名	unknown
7) wǔqì	武器	weapon
8) wǔlì	武力	military force
9) wǔyuè	五月	month of May
10) wǔxīng	五星	five-star
11) wǔfàn	午饭	lunch
12) kùzi	裤子	pants
13) wùhuì	误会	to misunderstand
14) wùlǐ	物理	physics
15) wùjià	物价	(commodity) price
16) gūlì	孤立	isolated
17) Tánggū	塘沽	(place name)
18) Zhūjiāng	珠江	(river name)
19) zūjīn	租金	rent
20) dúlì	独立	independent
21) dúshū	读书	to study
22) tòngkǔ	痛苦	pain, suffering
23) zǔguó	祖国	motherland
24) dùzi	肚子	stomach

Pronunciation Practice

🔊 Read the following words aloud. These name of fruits, vegetables and food can help you to practice your pronunciation of Chinese while learning those terms that are used every day in China.

1) shuǐguǒ 水果 fruit

2) lí 梨 pear

3) pútao 葡萄 grape

4) táo 桃 peach

5) lìzhī 荔枝 lichee

6) xiāngjiāo 香蕉 banana

7) píngguǒ 苹果 apple

8) júzi 桔子 orange

9) shūcài 蔬菜 vegetable

10) bōcài 菠菜 spinach

11) báicài 白菜 Chinese cabbage

12) tǔdòu 土豆 potato

13) biǎndòu 扁豆 green bean

14) xiǎocōng 小葱 green onion

15) qīngjiāo 青椒 green pepper

16) xīhóngshì 西红柿 tomato

17) shēngcài 生菜 lettuce

18) tiáoliào 调料 seasonings

19) yán 盐 salt

20) hújiāo 胡椒 pepper

21) báitáng 白糖 sugar

22) cù 醋 vinegar

23) jiàngyóu 酱油 soy sauce

24) guàntóu 罐头 canned food, tin

25) yóu 油 oil

26) làjiāojiàng 辣椒酱 chili sauce

27) shípǐn 食品 food

28) miànbāo 面包 bread

29) miànfěn 面粉 flour

30) mǐ 米 rice

31) miàntiáo 面条 noodle

32) bāozi 包子 steamed stuffed bun

33) jiǎozi 饺子 dumpling

34) rìyòngpǐn 日用品 household items

35) féizào 肥皂 soap

36) shūzi 梳子 comb

37) wèishēngzhǐ 卫生纸 toilet paper

38) jiǎnzi 剪子 scissors

39) xǐfàjì 洗发剂 shampoo

40) yáshuā 牙刷 toothbrush

41) máojīn 毛巾 towel

42) yágāo 牙膏 toothpaste

43) zhǐjiadāo 指甲刀 nail clippers

44) guāhúdāo 刮胡刀 razor

🔘 Read the following words aloud. These words can help you to practice your pronunciation of Chinese while learning some job titles that are used every day in China.

1) yóudìyuán 邮递员 postal worker

2) dǎgōngmèi 打工妹 farm girl working as a laborer in a city

3) xiǎoshígōng 小时工 hourly paid housekeeper

4) qīngjiégōng 清洁工 janitor

5) fù xiàozhǎng 副校长 vice-president, deputy head-master or headmistress

6) zǔzhǎng 组长 group leader

7) xuézhě 学者 scholar

8) bānzhǎng 班长 class leader

9) yánjiūshēng 研究生 graduate student

10) yánjiūyuán 研究员 research fellow

11) xìzhǔrèn 系主任 department chair

12) jiémù zhǔchírén 节目主持人 TV host

13) biānjì 编辑 editor

14) shèyǐngshī 摄影师 cameraman/camerawoman

15) shīrén 诗人 poet

Calendars: Part C

🔊 Read and listen to the dialogue, then answer the questions.

First review these new vocabulary words:

糟糕 zāogāo (terrible, unfortunate)

功课 gōngkè (homework)

什么时候 shénme shíhòu (what time)

时间 shíjiān (time)

快 kuài (hurry up)

A: 今天星期几？

B: 今天星期四。

A: 今天不是星期五吗？

B: 不是。今天不是星期五，今天是星期四。

A: 糟糕！今天我有中文课。我的功课还没做呢。

B: 你昨天为什么没做呢？

A: 昨天下课以后我去银行换钱了。回来以后又看了一会儿电视，就没做功课。

B: 今天你什么时候有中文课？

A: 今天下午两点我有中文课。现在几点了？

B: 现在是九点半。还有时间，你快做吧。

Questions:

1. What day is today? _____

_____

▶

2. What class does speaker "A" have today and at what time? _____

_____

_____

3. Does he have any problems with the class? _____

_____

_____

4. What time does this conversation take place? _____

_____

_____

Write the seven days of the week in Pinyin or characters in the blanks below.

Monday _____

Saturday _____

Tuesday _____

Friday _____

Wednesday _____

Sunday _____

Thursday _____

Exercise 2

Write the twelve months of the year in Pinyin or characters in the blanks below.

January_____

November _____

July _____

October _____

February_____

December_____

June _____

March _____

May _____

August _____

April _____

September _____

Write the month and date of the national day of Canada (July 1), the United States (July 4), the People's Republic of China (October 1) and Taiwan (October 10), in Pinyin or characters in the blanks below.

Canada: _____

United States: _____

People's Republic of China: _____

Taiwan:_____

Exercise 4

Translate the following phrases into Chinese and write them in Pinyin or characters in the blanks below.

1) Monday morning _____

2) Thursday at 3:30 P.M._____

3) July 4, 1776_____

4) May 1, 2001 _____

5) October 1, 1949 _____

6) Sunday afternoon _____

Exercise 5

Fill in the blanks in each sentence, paying attention to whether a measure word is needed.

1) _____ 年有 _____ 月 。
   (one)   nián yǒu   yuè.

2) _____ 月有 _____ 天 。
   (January) yuè yǒu   tiān.

Exercise 6

▶

257

3) _____ 星期有 _____ 天。
   (one)   xīngqī yǒu   tiān.

4) _____ 星期三是 _____ 月 _____ 号。
   (next)   xīngqīsān shì   yuè   hào.

5) _____ 年我是 _____ 岁。
   (this)   nián wǒ shì   suì.

6) _____ 月我去中国。
   (next)   yuè wǒ qù Zhōngguó.

7) 我 _____ 天有三节课。
   Wǒ _(every)_   tiān yǒu sān jié kè.

Exercise 7

To communicate in Chinese, you will need to talk about your schedule. To prepare, translate the following sentences into Chinese. Write the Chinese in Pinyin or characters.

1) Tomorrow is Friday. I have Chinese class in the afternoon._____

   _____

2) Do you teach English on Tuesday and Wednesday? ___

   _____

   _____

3) December 15th is my birthday. I want to celebrate my birthday in China._____

   _____

   _____

4) I do laundry every Saturday and watch TV on Sunday.

   _____

   _____

5) I will go to the Bank of China to exchange money on
   Monday. _____

   _____

   _____

| **Chinese Calendars** | Like much of the world, China uses the solar calendar (阳历 **yánglì**), based on the earth's rotation around the sun in 365 days. But the dates of traditional |

Chinese holidays are determined by the lunar calendar
(阴历 **yīnlì**), based on the moon's rotation around the
earth in 29 or 30 days, with 12 months a year, for a total
of 354 days. Chinese solar calendars usually have the
lunar calendar information in small print.

Qínhuái River in Nánjīng

Chinese Birth Signs (生肖 *shēngxiāo*)

Twelve animals, representing the twelve Earthly Branches, are used to symbolize the year in which a person is born. Traditionally, it is believed that birth signs reflect one's personality and influence the choice of a spouse. When you look up your birth sign, remember to use your birth year according to the lunar calendar, which begins in late January or February of the solar calendar.

鼠 shǔ (mouse)	1996 1984 1972 1960 1948 1936
牛 niú (ox)	1997 1985 1973 1961 1949 1937
虎 hǔ (tiger)	1998 1986 1974 1962 1950 1938
兔 tù (rabbit)	1999 1987 1975 1963 1951 1939
龙 lóng (dragon)	2000 1988 1976 1964 1952 1940
蛇 shé (snake)	2001 1989 1977 1965 1953 1941
马 mǎ (horse)	2002 1990 1978 1966 1954 1942
羊 yáng (sheep)	2003 1991 1979 1967 1955 1943
猴 hóu (monkey)	2004 1992 1980 1968 1956 1944
鸡 jī (rooster)	2005 1993 1981 1969 1957 1945
狗 gǒu (dog)	2006 1994 1982 1970 1958 1946
猪 zhū (pig)	2007 1995 1983 1971 1959 1947

Traditional Chinese Festivals

There are several traditional Chinese festivals:

LANTERN FESTIVAL (元宵节 **Yuánxiāojié**), on the fifteenth day of the Lunar New Year (in January or February), marks the end of the Spring Festival. People hang lanterns and eat boiled stuffed dumplings made of rice flour (汤圆 **tāngyuán**).

QINGMING FESTIVAL (清明节 **Qīngmíngjié**), on April 5, is for mourning one's ancestors. Traditional activities include sweeping off the graves of ancestors, offering sacrificial foods, and burning pieces of paper that resemble money for the dead to spend in their world.

DRAGON BOAT FESTIVAL (端午节 **Duānwǔjié**), on the fifth day of the fifth month in the lunar calendar (in April or May), commemorates the death of **Qū Yuán** (475–221 BC), the father of Chinese poetry. People eat sticky-rice dumplings steamed in lotus leaves (粽子 **zòngzi**). Some areas also have dragon boat races.

MID-AUTUMN FESTIVAL (中秋节 **Zhōngqiūjié**), on the fifteenth day of the eighth month in the lunar calendar (in September or October), commemorates an unsuccessful rebellion against the Mongolian rulers of the Yuan Dynasty (1271–1368). It is a festival for family reunions. On the eve of Mid-Autumn Festival, after eating dinner people watch the moon while eating "moon cakes" (月饼 **yuèbing**) and fruits.

Answer Key

Exercise 1:

1) China	Zhōngguó	2) Hong Kong	Xiānggǎng
3) Singapore	Xīnjiāpō	4) Sweden	Ruìdiǎn
5) Korea	Cháoxiǎn	6) Japan	Rìběn
7) Switzerland	Ruìshì	8) Canada	Jiānádà
9) Spain	Xībānyá	10) Scotland	Sūgélán

Exercise 2:

1) Xī' ān 西安
2) Wǔhàn 武汉
3) Nánjīng 南京
4) Guìlín 桂林
5) Chéngdōu 成都
6) Chángchūn 长春
7) Wūlǔmùqí 乌鲁木齐
8) Shényáng 沈阳
9) Shíjiāzhuāng 石家庄
10) Zhèngzhōu 郑州
11) Héféi 合肥
12) Nánchāng 南昌
13) Chángshā 长沙
14) Hángzhōu 杭州
15) Tàiyuán 太原
16) Fúzhōu 福州
17) Guǎngzhōu 广州
18) Kūnmíng 昆明
19) Guìyáng 贵阳
20) Nánníng 南宁
21) Lánzhōu 兰州
22) Xīníng 西宁
23) Lāsà 拉萨 (Lhasa)
24) Yínchuān 银川
25) Shēnzhèn 深圳
26) Sūzhōu 苏州

Exercise 3: Refer to the CD to check your pronunciation.

Exercise 4:

1) Yīngguó (England)
2) Yángzhōu (a city)
3) Mr. Wáng
4) Wǒ (I, me)
5) Yuènán (Vietnam)
6) yě (also)
7) xuéxí (to study)
8) wèi (hello)
9) yī (one)
10) yuán (¥1.00)
11) yǒu (to have)
12) yīn-yáng (the two opposing principles in nature)

Exercise 5: 1) Yǒuyì Shāngdiàn (Friendship Store)
2) Hǎidiàn (a district in Beijing)
3) Gùgōng (Palace Museum)
4) Tiānānmén (Square, Beijing)
5) Tiāntán (Temple of Heaven)
6) Hóngqiáo Shìchǎng (Pearl Market, Beijing)
7) Xiùshuǐ Dōngjiē (Silk Market, Beijing)
8) Yíhéyuán (Summer Palace)
9) Chángchéng (Great Wall)
10) Shísānlíng (Ming Tombs)
11) dàshǐguǎn (embassy)
12) Pānjiāyuán ("Mud Market," Beijing)

Lesson 6

Exercise 1: 1) shíyī   2) shígī
3) qīshíyī   4) sānshíliù
5) wǔshíjiǔ   6) jiǔshíjiǔ
7) sìshísì   8) yìbǎilíngyī
9) bābǎiyìshíèr   10) yìbǎi líng sān

Exercise 2: 1) 三加六是几？ <u>9</u> Sān jiā liù shì jiǔ.
2) 十加十是几？ <u>20</u> Shí jiā shí shì èrshí.
3) 七加七是几？ <u>14</u> Qī jiā qī shì shísì.
4) 五十加五十是几？ <u>100</u> Wǔ shí jiā wǔ shí shì yìbǎi.
5) 四十五加六十六是几？ <u>111</u> Sì shí sì jiā liù shíliù
shì yìbǎi yìshí yī.

Exercise 3: 1) <u>12</u>   2) <u>64</u>   3) <u>38</u>   4) <u>57</u>
5) <u>89</u>   6) <u>96</u>   7) <u>101</u>   8) <u>224</u>
9) <u>756</u>   10) <u>984</u>

Exercise 4: 6: liù   1: yī   7: qī   3: sān
8: bā   5: wǔ   9: jiǔ   10: shí

Exercise 5: 1) ♦ ♦ ♦ ♦ + ♦ ♦ ♦ ♦ ♦ = 9 sì jiā wǔ shì jiǔ 四加五
是九

2) ♦ ♦ ♦ ♦ ♦ ♦ ♦ + ♦ ♦ ♦ ♦ ♦ ♦ ♦= 14 qī jiā qī shì
shí sì 七加七是十四

3) ♦ ♦ ♦ ♦ + ♦ ♦ ♦ ♦ = 8 sì jiā sì shì bā 四加四是八

4) ♦ ♦ ♦ + ♦ ♦ ♦ ♦ ♦ ♦ ♦ ♦ = 11 sān jiā bā
shì shí yī 三加八是十一

5) ♦ ♦ ♦ ♦ ♦ ♦ + ♦ ♦ ♦ ♦ ♦ ♦ ♦ = 13 liù jiā qī shì
shí sān 六加七是十三

6) ♦ ♦ ♦ ♦ ♦ + ♦ ♦ ♦ ♦ ♦ ♦ = 11 wǔ jiā liù shì shí
yī 五加六是十一

7) ♦ ♦ ♦ ♦ ♦ + ♦ ♦ = 7 wǔ jiā 'èr shì qī 五加二是七

Exercise 1: 1) What did the foreigner want to do? <u>Exchange
money</u>

2) What kind of currency and what amount did he
want to exchange at the bank? <u>He wanted to
exchange $200 into RMB</u>

3) What amount did he receive? <u>1,660 RMB</u>

4) How much RMB equals one U.S. dollar? <u>8.20
RMB = $1.00</u>

Exercise 2: 1) Which item did the American want? <u>That one</u>

2) How much did he pay the clerk? <u>2.50 yuan</u>

3) What did the clerk say after he gave her the
money? <u>OK</u>

Exercise 3: 1) liǎng kuài   5) liǎng máo

2) liǎng fēn   6) liǎng bǎi

3) liǎng yuán   7) liǎng jiǎo

4) liǎng qiān   8) liǎng Měiyuán

Exercise 4: 37 sānshíqī   56 wǔshíliù
94 jiǔshísì   27 èrshíqī
19 shíjiǔ   65 liùshíwǔ
12 shí'èr   73 qīshísān
100 yìbǎi   109 yìbǎi líng jiǔ
123 yìbǎi èrshísān   176 yìbǎi qīshí liù

Exercise 1:
1) What does the foreigner ask for first? <u>Steamed bread</u>
2) What else does the foreigner ask for? <u>Rice</u>
3) How much is the total cost? <u>3.00 yuan</u>
4) The change the foreigner receives back is <u>2.00 yuan</u>

Exercise 2:
1) How many dishes does the foreigner order? <u>Two</u>
2) How much is the total bill? <u>5.00 yuan</u>

Exercise 4:
1) fish <u>yú</u>   2) chicken <u>jī</u>
3) noodles <u>miàntiáo</u>   4) beef <u>ròu</u>

Exercise 5:
1) Is this a beef dish?
这是牛肉吗?
Zhè shì niúròu ma?

2) I don't want this dish. I want that dish.
我不要这个菜。我要那个菜。
Wǒ bú yào zhè ge cài. Wǒ yào nà ge cài.

3) I would like egg-drop soup.
我要鸡蛋汤。
Wǒ yào jīdàntāng.

4) I also want four steamed buns.
我还要四个馒头。
Wǒ hái yào sì mántou.

5) I don't want any more, thank you.
不要了，谢谢。
Búyào le, xièxie.

Lesson 15

Exercise 1:   1) What did the customer ask the waiter first?   <u>What dishes do you have?</u>

2) What did the customer ask the waiter after that?   <u>What kind of meat dishes do you have?</u>

3) What order did the customer finally order?   <u>Lamb</u>

Exercise 2:   1) What did the waiter ask the customer?   <u>What would you like to drink?</u>

2) What beverage did the waiter offer?   <u>Beer, coke and tea</u>

3) What did the customer want?   <u>A pot of tea</u>

Exercise 3:   free answers

Exercise 4:   1) What dishes do you have?

你们有什么菜？

Nǐmen yǒu shéme cài?

2) Two of us are vegetarians. Do you have vegetarian dishes?

我们都吃素。有素菜吗？

Wǒmen dōu chīsù.Yǒu sùcài ma?

3) Please bring us two glasses of beer, one cola, and one water. (来 lái)

请来两杯啤酒，一杯可乐，一杯水。

Qǐng lái liǎng bēi píjiǔ, yì bēi kělě, yì bēi shuǐ.

4) We would like to order three dishes: one quick-fried beef with onions, one fish, and one vegetable dish.

我们要三个菜：一个葱爆牛肉，一个鱼和一个素菜。

Wǒmen yào sān ge cài: yí ge cōngbào niúròu, yí yú hé yí ge sùcài.

5) Miss, the check please. How much is it altogether? (一共 yígòng)

小姐，买单。一共多少钱？

Xiǎojie, mǎidān. Yígòng duōshao qián?

Exercise 1:   1) rìběn 日本

2 rènào 热闹

3) réngrán 仍然

4) róngyì 容易

5) ránhòu 然后

6) ràngbù 让步

7) rénkǒu 人口

8) rènwéi 认为

9) tūrán 突然

10) chuanrǎn 传染

11) róngrěn 容忍

12) ruǎnruò 软弱

13) zìrán 自然

14) huāruǐ 花蕊

15) zérèn 责任

Exercise 2:   1) What is the rate for a call to the United States?

<u>3.50 yuan per minute</u>

2) What is the rate for a call to Japan?   <u>2.00 yuan per</u>
<u>minute</u>

3) What is the cheaper way to call?   <u>Use a phone card</u>

Exercise 3:   1) 银行   <u>yínháng</u>

2) 服务员   <u>fúwùyuán</u>

3) 宾馆   <u>bīnguǎn</u>

4) 402 房间   <u>sìlíngèr fángjiān</u>

5) 打电话   <u>dǎ diànhuà</u>

6) 在不在   <u>zài bùzài</u>

7) 回电话   <u>huí diànhuà</u>

8) 告诉   <u>gàosu</u>

9) 不客气   <u>bùkèqi</u>

10) 您找谁   <u>nín zhǎo shéi</u>

Exercise 4:   1) 我买一张 IP 卡。Wǒ mǎi yì zhāng kǎ.

2) 我换一百块钱。Wǒ huàn yìbǎi kuài qián.

3) 你要什么菜？我要一个鸡，三个馒头。Nǐ yào
shénme cài? Wǒ yào yí gè jī, sān gè mántou.

Exercise 5:   1) 一共多少钱？Yígòng duōshao qián?

2) 在哪儿买电话卡？Zài nǎr mǎi diànhuàkǎ?

3) 你们有什么菜？Nímen yǒu shénme cài?

4) 请问，马丽莎在吗？Qǐng wèn, Mǎ Lìshā zài ma?

Exercise 6: 1) How can I make a phone call to the United States?

怎么给美国打电话？

Zěma gěi Měiguo dǎdiànhuà?

2) What number should I dial first?

我先拨什么号？

Wǒ xiān bōshénme hào?

3) How much is it per minute to call the United States?

给美国打电话多少钱一分钟？

Gěi Měiguo dǎdiànhuà duōshǎo qián yì fēnzhōng?

4) That's too expensive. Where can I buy a phone card?

太贵了。在哪儿买电话卡？

Tài guìle. Zài nǎr mǎi diànhuàkǎ?

Exercise 1:

1) nǔlì (努力)	2) nǔshì (女士)
3) nǔxìng (女性)	4) núlì (奴隶)
5) Lǔ Xùn (鲁迅)	6) lǜshī (律师)
7) lǘzi (驴子)	8) lúzi (炉子)
9) fǎlǜ (法律)	10) mǎlù (马路)
11) fùnǚ (妇女)	12) mìlǔ (秘鲁)
13) fènnù (愤怒)	14) kǎolǜ (考虑)
15) bùjué rúlǚ (不绝如缕)	

Exercise 2: 1) The room number of the female foreigner is 302.

True

2) The male foreigner's room is in good condition.

False

3) The female foreigner needs towels and clean sheets.

False

4) The attendant will send towels and change the sheets.

True

Exercise 3: 1) towels máojīn   2) soap féizào

3) toilet paper wèishēngzhǐ   4) hanger yījià

Exercise 4: 1) I need one roll of toilet paper and three hangers.

我需要一卷 (juǎn - roll) 卫生纸和三个衣架。

Wǒ xūyào yí juǎn wèishēngzhǐ hé sān ge yījià.

2) My lamp is broken.

我的灯坏了。

Wǒde dēng huàile.

3) Who is it? Please come back later.

谁？请等一会儿再来。

Shéi? Qǐng děng yí huìr zàií.

4) Please clean my room now. Could you change my sheets?

请现在打扫我的房间。能换床单吗？

Qǐng xiànzài dǎsǎo wǒde fángjiān le. Néng huàn chuángdān ma?

5) Please send one bar of soap and two towels to my room. I am staying in room 312. Thanks.

请给我送一块肥皂，两条毛巾来。我住 312 房间。谢谢。

Qǐng gěi wǒ sòng yī kuài féizào, liǎng tiáo máojīn lái. Wǒ zhù sì wǔ fángjiān. Xièxie.

Exercise 1: 1) <u>tàijí</u> 太极

2) <u>zhīshi</u> 支使

3) <u>zhīshi</u> 知识

4) <u>shízǐ</u> 石子

5) <u>sīzì</u> 私自

6) <u>jīqi</u> 机器

7) <u>shísì búshì sìshí</u> 十四不是四十

8) <u>shí zhǐ bù yī</u> 十指不一

9) <u>jījí nǔlì</u> 积极努力

10) <u>shí shì qiú shì</u> 实事求是

Exercise 2: 1) What does the English person want? <u>To find out</u>
<u>something.</u>
2) What is the English person looking for? <u>The library.</u>
3) On which side of the library is the movie theatre?
<u>The right side.</u>

Exercise 3:

1) 商店旁边是书店。 (有) → 商店旁边有书店。
Shāngdiàn pángbian shì (yǒu) Shāngdiàn pángbian yǒu
shūdiàn. shūdiàn.

2) 英文系在教学楼旁边。 (是) → 英文系旁边是教学楼。
Yīngwénxì zài jiàoxuélóu (shì) Yīngwénxì pángbian shì
pángbian. jiàoxuélóu.

3) 银行旁边是邮局。 (在) → 邮局在银行旁边。
Yínháng pángbian shì (zài) Yóujú zài yínháng páng-
yóujú. bian.

4) 食堂在七号楼旁边。 (是) → 食堂旁边是七号楼。
Shítáng zài qīhàolóu (shì) Shítáng pángbian shì
pángbian. qīhàolóu.

5) 马路对面是中国银行。 (有) → 马路对面有中国银行。
Mǎlù duìmiàn shì (yǒu) Mǎ lù duìmiàn yǒu
Zhōngguó Yínháng. Zhōngguó Yínháng.

6) 书店后面有一个厕所。 (在) → 厕所在书店后面。
Shūdiàn hòumiàn yǒu yí (zài) Cèsuǒ zài shūdiàn hòu-
ge cèsuǒ. mian.

Exercise 4: 1) Where is the bathroom?
厕所在哪儿?
Cèsuǒ zài nǎr?
2) Where is the English Department? It is behind the
classroom building.
英文系在哪儿? 在教学楼后边。
Yīngwénxì zài nǎr? Zài jiàoxuélóu hòubian.
3) How can I get to the Bank of China? Go straight,
and then turn left.
我怎么走中国银行? 一直走、再左转。

Wǒ zěnme zǒu Zhōnggó Yinháng? Yìzhí zǒu, zài zuǒ zhuǎn.

4) Is there an Internet cafe around here? The Internet cafe is on the left side of the gate.
附近有网吧吗？网吧在大门左边。
Fùjìn yǒu wǎngbā ma? Wǎngbā zài dàmén zuǒbian.

5) Is it far? How can I get there?
远吗？我怎么走？
Yuǎn ma? Wǒ zěnme zuǒ.

6) Excuse me, where is the bookstore? First go straight, pass the Bank of China, and then turn left.
请问，书店在哪儿？先一直走，经过中国银行，再左转。
Qǐng wen, shūdiàn zài nǎr? Xiān yìzhí zǒu, jīngguo Zhōngguó Yínháng, zài zuǒ zhuǎn.

7) Is the hospital across the street from the main gate?
医院是在大门对面吗？
Yīyuàn shì dàmén duìmiàn ma?

8) The post office is not far. It is over there.
邮局不远。
Yóujú bú yuǎn.

Exercise 1:

1) 捐款	juānkuǎn	2) 句子	jùzi
3) 柱子	zhùzi	4) 完全	wánquán
5) 转变	zhuǎnbiàn	6) 猪圈	zhūjuàn
7) 请求	qǐngqiú	8) 顺利	shùnlì
9) 英雄	yīngxióng	10) 通讯	tōngxùn
11) 长江	Chángjiāng	12) 追究	zhuījiū
13) 水渠	shuǐqú	14) 权力	quánlì
15) 接触	jiēchù	16) 拒绝	jùjué
17) 出去	chūqu	18) 居住	jūzhù

19) 专制　zhuānzhì　　　20) 追求　zhuīqiú

Exercise 2:　1) What time does this conversation take place?　<u>8:00 am</u>

2) What time does the bank open?　<u>It opens at 9:00 am</u>

3) Why does the American want to go to the bank?
<u>He wants to exchange money.</u>

4) Where is the bank located?　<u>It is next to the book-store.</u>

Exercise 3:　2:00 p.m.　xiàwǔ liǎng diǎn　下午两点

4:10 p.m.　xiàwǔ sì diǎn shí fēn　下午四点十分

6:15 p.m.　xiàwǔ liù diǎn yīkè　下午六点一刻

9:45 a.m.　shàngwǔ jiǔ diǎn sānkè　上午九点三刻

10:05 a.m.　shàngwǔ shí diǎn líng wǔ　上午十点零五

11:00 a.m.　shàngwǔ shíyī diǎn　上午十一点

8:30 a.m.　zǎoshàng bā diǎn bàn　早上八点半

7:10 a.m.　zǎoshàng qī diǎn shí fēn　早上七点十分

12:00 p.m.　zhōngwǔ shí 'èr diǎn　中午十二点

3:50 p.m.　xià wǔ chà shí fēn sì diǎn　下午差十分四点

5:55 p.m.　xiàwǔ chà wǔ fēn liù diǎn　下午差五分六点

1:00 p.m.　xià wǔ yì diǎn　下午一点

Exercise 4:　1) 你早上<u>几点</u> 起床？

Nǐ zǎoshang jǐdiǎn qǐchuáng?

2) 下课以后你做<u>什么</u>？

Xiàkè yǐhòu nǐ zuò shénme?

3) 你跟<u>谁</u>一起去商店？

Nǐ gēn shuí yìqǐ qù shāngdiàn?

4) 晚上我去找你，<u>好吗</u>？

Wǎnshang wǒ qù zhǎo nǐ, hǎo ma?

5) 电话卡<u>多少钱</u>一张？

Diànhuàkǎ duōshao qián yì zhāng?

6) 厕所在<u>哪儿</u>？　Cèsuǒ zài nǎr?

7) 你下午上班<u>吗</u>？　Nǐ xiàwǔ shàngbān ma?

Exercise 5:　1) What time is it now? It is five to ten.

现在几点？现在差五分十点。

Xiànzài jǐ diǎn? Xiànzài chà wǔ fēn shí diǎn.

2) Shall we go to dinner together tonight?

晚上我们一起去吃饭，好吗？

Wǎnshang wǒmen yìqǐ qù chīfàn, hǎo ma?

3) What are you doing today? I am going to the Internet cafe after teaching English.

你今天做什么？下英文课以后我去网吧。

Nǐ jīntian zuò shénme? Xià Yīngwén kè yǐhòu wǒ qù wǎngbā.

4) It is a quarter to four now. I will take a rest.

现在差一刻四点。我休息一会儿。

Xiànzài chà yí kè sì diǎn. Wǒ xiūxi yí huìr.

5) When do you go to bed everyday? I often go to bed at 11:00 p.m.

你每天几点睡觉？我常常晚上十一点睡觉。

Nǐ jǐ diǎn shuìjiào? Wǒ chángcháng wǎnshang shíyī diǎn shuìjiào.

6) Sometimes I take a shower in the morning, sometimes in the evening.

我有时候早上洗澡，有时候晚上洗澡。

Wǒ yǒushíhou zǎoshang xǐzǎo, yǒushíhou wǎnshang xǐzǎo.

7) I go to class in the morning, and go to work in the afternoon.

我上午上中文课，下午上班。

Wǒ shàngwǔ shàngkè, xiàwǔ shàngbān.

8) I get off work at 5:00 p.m.

我下午五点下班。

Wǒ xiàwǔ wǔ diǎn xiàbān.

Exercise 1:   1) What day is today?   <u>Thursday</u>

2) What class does speaker "A" have today and at what time? <u>He has Chinese class at 2:00 p.m. today.</u>

3) Does he have any problems with the class? <u>He forgot to do the homework.</u>

4) What time does this conversation take place? <u>9:30 a.m.</u>

Exercise 2: Monday <u>xīngqīyī 星期一</u>

Saturday <u>xīngqīliù 星期六</u>

Tuesday <u>xīngqī'èr 星期二</u>

Friday <u>xīngqīwǔ 星期五</u>

Wednesday <u>xīngqīsān 星期三</u>

Sunday <u>xīngqīrì / xīngqītiān 星期日 / 星期天</u>

Thursday <u>xīngqīsì 星期四</u>

Exercise 3: January <u>yíyuè 一月</u>

November <u>shíyīyuè 十一月</u>

July <u>qīyuè 七月</u>

October <u>shíyuè 十月</u>

February <u>èryuè 二月</u>

December <u>shí'èryuè 十二月</u>

June <u>liùyuè 六月</u>

March <u>sānyuè 三月</u>

May <u>wǔyuè 五月</u>

August <u>bāyuè 八月</u>

April <u>sìyuè 四月</u>

September <u>jiǔyuè 九月</u>

Exercise 4: Canada: <u>qīyuè yí hào 七月一号</u>

United States: <u>qīyuè sì hào 七月四号</u>

People's Republic of China: <u>shíyuè yí hào 十月一号</u>

Taiwan: <u>shíyuè shí hào 十月十号</u>

Exercise 5: 1) Monday morning <u>xīngqīyī shàngwǔ 星期一上午</u>

2) Thursday at 3:30 p.m. <u>xīngqīsì xiàwǔ sān diǎn bàn 星期四下午三点半</u>

3) July 4, 1776 <u>yī qī qī liù nián qīyuè sì hào 一七七</u>

六年七月四号

4) May 1, 2001　èr ling ling yī nián wǔyuè yí hào 二
零零年五月一号

5) October 1, 1949　yī jiǔ sì jiǔ nián shíyuè yí hào 一
九四九年十月一号

6) Sunday afternoon　xīngqīrì xiàwǔ 星期日下午

Exercise 6:　1) 一年有十二个月。
yì nián yǒu shí'èr ge yuè.

2)) 一月有三十一天。
yí yuè yǒu sānshíyī tiān.

3) 一个星期有七天。
yí ge xīngqī yǒu qī tiān.

4) 下个星期三是三月十六号。
xià ge xīngqīsān shì sān yuè shíliù hào.

5) 今年我是二十岁。
jīnnián wǒ shì èrshí suì.

6) 下个月我去中国。
xià ge yuè wǒ qù Zhōngguó.

7) 我每天有三节课。
Wǒ měi tiān yǒu sān jié kè.

Exercise 7:　1) Tomorrow is Friday. I have Chinese class in the
afternoon.
明天是星期五。我下午有中文课。
Míngtiān shì xīngqīwǔ. Wǒ xiàwǔ yǒu Zhóngwén
kè.

2) Do you teach English on Tuesday and Wednesday?
你星期二，星期三教英语吗？
Nǐ xīngqī'èr, xīngqīsān jiāo Yīngyǔ ma?

3) December 15th is my birthday. I will celebrate my
birthday in China.
十二月十五号是我的生日。我想在中国过生日。
Shí'èr yuè shí wǔ hào shì wǒde shēngrì. Wǒ xiǎng

zài Zhōngguò.

4) I do laundry every Saturday and watch TV on Sunday.

我每个星期六都洗衣服，星期日看电视。

Wǒ měi ge xīngqīliù dòu xǐ yīfu, xīngqīrì kàn diànshì.

5) I will go to the Bank of China to exchange money on Monday.

星期一我去中国银行换钱。

Xīngqīyī wǒ qù Zhōngguó Yínháng huàn qián.

Vocabulary List

Characters	Pinyin	English
B		
八	bā	eight
吧	bā	bar, cafe
吧	ba	(to make a mild imperative, to imply agreement or a degree of certainty, to express unwillingness or hesitation)
白	bái	white; plain
百	bǎi	hundred
班	bān	class; shift; regularly-run
半	bàn	half, partly
拌	bàn	to stir and mix (with sauce)
办	bàn	to manage, to handle, to set up
镑	bàng	pound
办公室	bàngōngshì	office
爆	bào	to quick-fry; to explode
八月	bāyuè	August
杯	bēi	cup, glass
北	běi	north

Characters	Pinyin	English
北京	Běijīng	Beijing
杯子	bēizi	cup
币	bì	currency, money, coin
边	biān	side, edge
表	biǎo	form, chart
别	bié	difference; don't
宾	bīn	guest
宾馆	bīnguǎn	hotel, guesthouse
冰	bīng	ice, to freeze
饼	bǐng	fried bread
拨	bō	to dial
不	bù	no, not
步	bù	a step; to go on foot, to walk
不对	búduì	incorrect, wrong
不客气	búkèqi	You're welcome.
不是	búshì	No, it is not.
不谢	búxie	Not at all. / You're welcome.

C

菜	cài	dish; vegetable
菜单	càidān	menu

Characters	Pinyin	English
餐	cān	meal; to eat
操	cāo	to operate; exercise
厕	cè	toilet
厕所	cèsuǒ	bathroom, toilet
茶	chá	tea
差	chà	short of, wanting; to differ from
常常	chángcháng	often
炒	chǎo	to stir-fry
炒鸡蛋	chǎojīdàn	scrambled eggs
炒鸡丁	chǎojīdīng	stir-fried diced chicken with diced vegetables
叉子	chāzi	fork
吃	chī	to eat
吃饭	chīfàn	to eat a meal
吃素	chīsù	to eat only vegetables (vegetarian)
出	chū	to go out, exit; to appear
初	chū	beginning, elementary
出生	chūshēng	to be born
床	chuáng	bed

Characters	Pinyin	English
床单	chuángdān	bed sheets
春	chūn	spring
此	cǐ	here, this
葱	cōng	green onion
葱爆	cōngbào	quick-fry with green onions
醋	cù	vinegar

D

打	dǎ	to make (a phone call); to hit, to beat; to play (ball)
打电话	dǎdiànhuà	to make a phone call
打扫	dǎsǎo	to clean, to sweep
大	dà	big, large, major; age
大门	dàmén	main entrance
大学	dàxué	university, college
单	dān	single, bill
蛋	dàn	egg
道	dào	road, channel
的	de	(function word)
灯	dēng	light, lamp
等	děng	to wait

Characters	Pinyin	English
地	dì	earth, locality, field
第	dì	(indicates an ordinal number)
地区	dìqū	area, region
点	diǎn	o'clock; (decimal) point; to choose, to mark
店	diàn	shop, store
电	diàn	electricity; electric
电话	diànhuà	telephone
电话卡	diànhuàkǎ	telephone card
电视	diànshì	television
电影	diànyǐng	movie
丁	dīng	cube, diced piece
东	dōng	east
都	dōu	all, both
豆	dòu	beans, peas
对	duì	right, correct; opposite
兑	duì	to exchange, to convert
兑换单	duìhuàndān	exchange form
对面	duìmiàn	on the opposite side, across the street
多大	duōdà	How old?

Characters	Pinyin	English
多少	duōshao	How many? How much?

E

二	èr	two

F

法学院	fǎxuéyuàn	law school
翻译	fānyì	translator, interpreter; to translate, to interpret
饭	fàn	meal; cooked rice
饭馆(儿)	fànguǎnr	restaurant
房	fáng	room, house
房间	fángjiān	room
肥皂	féizào	soap
分	fēn	¥0.01, cent; minute
分钟	fēnzhōng	minute
腐	fǔ	bean curd; to decay
附近	fùjìn	nearby; in the vicinity of, closely

G

港	gǎng	port; Hong Kong (short form of 香港 Xiānggǎng)

Characters	Pinyin	English
港币	Gǎngbì	Hong Kong dollar (HK$)
告诉	gàosu	to tell, to inform, to let know
个	ge/gè	(measure word for people or things, and can be used to replace some other measure words)
给	gěi	to, for (when transferring something to someone); to give
跟	gēn	with
工	gōng	work; worker; skill
公	gōng	public, state-owned
宫保	gōngbǎo	a spicy, diced meat dish
公司	gōngsī	company, corporation, firm
工作	gōngzuò	to work; work, job
瓜	guā	melon, gourd
馆	guǎn	shop, hall
贵	guì	expensive, valuable, honored
贵姓	guì xìng	Your surname, please?
国	guó	country
过	guò	to pass, to cross, to go through; to celebrate; to spend (time)
过生日	guò shēngri	to celebrate a birthday

Characters	Pinyin	English
H		
还	hái	in addition, still, yet
寒	hán	cold
汉	hàn	Chinese
汉语	Hànyǔ	Chinese language
好	hǎo	good, well, OK
好吧	hǎo ba	OK, all right
好吗	hǎo ma	Is it OK? Shall we?
号	hào	number, size; date
行	háng/xíng	line, profession; to walk; OK
喝	hē	to drink
和	hé	and
很	hěn	very, very much
红	hóng	red; symbol of luck
后	hòu	rear, back, the latter; behind, after
后边	hòubian	back, rear
后天	hòutiān	the day after tomorrow
护	hù	to guard, to protect
护照	hùzhào	passport
花	huā	flower; to spend

Characters	Pinyin	English
话	huà	word; to talk
坏	huài	bad, broken, to become spoiled
坏了	huài le	to be out of order, to become spoiled
换	huàn	to exchange, to trade, to change
黄	huáng	yellow
回	huí	to return, to go back
婚	hūn	marriage; to wed

J

机	jī	machine, engine; opportunity
鸡	jī	chicken
几	jǐ	How many?; a few, several
加	jiā	to add; plus
家	jiā	home, family
假	jiǎ/jià	false; holiday, vacation
间	jiān	room; between
见	jiàn	to meet, to see, to call on
酱	jiàng	soy bean sauce, sauce, jam; cooked in soy sauce
教	jiāo/jiào	to teach

Characters	Pinyin	English
椒	jiāo	hot pepper plant
角	jiǎo	¥0.10; corner, horn
饺	jiǎo	dumpling with vegetable and meat stuffing
叫	jiào	to be called, to call out
教学楼	jiàoxuélóu	classroom building
鸡蛋	jīdàn	egg
鸡蛋汤	jīdàntāng	egg-drop soup
鸡丁	jīdīng	diced chicken
几点	jǐdiǎn	What time?
几号	jǐhào	What date (of the month)? What number?
街	jiē	street
节	jié	section, segment, period (of a class); festival, holiday
今	jīn	the present, today
今年	jīnnián	this year
今天	jīntiān	today
进	jìn	to enter, to come in
禁	jìn	to forbid; prohibition
京	jīng	capital; Beijing

Characters	Pinyin	English
经过	jīngguò	to pass by, to pass through
境	jìng	border, territory, condition
九	jiǔ	nine
酒	jiǔ	liquor, wine
桔	jú	orange, tangerine
局	jú	bureau; gathering

K

咖啡	kāfēi	coffee
卡	kǎ	card
开	kāi	to open; to set out; to turn on, to operate
看	kàn/kān	to watch, to see; to look after
可	kě	co(la) (first character of 可乐 kělè); but; can, may
可乐	kělè	cola (short for 可口可乐 Kěkǒu Kělè)
可能	kěnéng	may, might; possible
可以	kěyǐ	may, can; may be permitted to
课	kè	class, course
刻	kè	quarter of an hour, 15 minutes; a quarter

Characters	*Pinyin*	*English*
块	kuài	¥1.00 (colloquial form of 元 yuán), dollar; (measure word for things in chunks or solid pieces); chunk
筷子	kuàizi	chopsticks

L

辣	là	spicy, hot
来	lái	to bring; to come; to arrive
了	le	(indicates a change of situation or completed action)
乐	lè	(co)la (second character of 可乐 kělè); happy
冷	lěng	cold, frosty
冷饮	lěngyǐn	cold drink(s)
里	lǐ	inside, inner; a Chinese unit of length
凉	liáng	cool; cold
两	liǎng	two; a few
料	liào	material, ingredient
零	líng	zero
龄	líng	age, duration

Characters	*Pinyin*	*English*
留学生	liúxuéshēng	student studying abroad, foreign student
六	liù	six
楼	lóu	multi-story building; story, floor
路	lù	road; route, journey
绿	lǜ	green

M

吗	ma	(forms a question)
马	mǎ	horse
买	mǎi	to buy
卖	mài	to sell
买单	mǎidān	bill/check (in a restaurant or bar)
马路	mǎlù	road, street
馒头	mántou	steamed bread, steamed bun
毛	máo	¥0.10 (colloquial of 角 jiǎo); a surname
毛巾	máojīn	towel
没	méi	not; to not have (short form of 没有 méiyǒu)
没有	méiyǒu	to not have

Characters	Pinyin	English
每	měi	every, each
每个	měige	every, each
每个星期	měi ge xīngqī	every week, weekly
每天	měi tiān	every day
美	měi	beautiful; America (short form of 美国 Měiguó)
美国	Měiguó	United States
美国人	Měiguórén	American (person)
美元	Měiyuán	U.S. currency, dollar
门	mén	entrance, door, gate
米	mǐ	uncooked rice; meter
面	miàn	noodle, flour
面条	miàntiáo	noodles
米饭	mǐfàn	cooked rice
民	mín	people, citizen
明	míng	tomorrow, next; bright
名	míng	name; fame
明年	míngnián	next year
明天	míngtiān	tomorrow
末	mò	end; powder; last

Characters	*Pinyin*	*English*
N		
哪	nǎ	Which? What?
哪个	nǎge	Which? Which one?
哪年	nǎnián	Which year?
哪儿	nǎr	Where?
那	nà/nèi	that
那个	nà ge/nèi ge	that one
那儿	nàr	there
奶	nǎi	milk, breast
男	nán	man, male
南	nán	south
呢	ne	how about (you, this, that)?
内	nèi	inside, inner
能	néng	can; to be able to
你	nǐ	you
你的	nǐ de	yours
你好	nǐ hǎo	Hello! How do you do!
你们	nǐmen	you (plural)
年	nián	year
您	nín	you (polite form)

Characters	*Pinyin*	*English*
您的	nínde	yours (polite form)
牛	niú	cow
牛肉	niúròu	beef
女	nǚ	woman, female

O

欧	ōu	Europe (short form of 欧洲 Ōuzhōu)

P

盘子	pánzi	plate
旁	páng	side; nearby; other
旁边	pángbian	side; beside, nearby
朋友	péngyou	friend
啤	pí	beer
啤酒	píjiǔ	beer
片	piàn	slice, thin piece
瓶	píng	bottle

Q

七	qī	seven
期	qī	period; to expect

Characters	Pinyin	English
起床	qǐchuáng	to get up
汽车站	qìchēzhàn	bus stop
千	qiān	thousand
签	qiān	to sign; a label
签字	qiānzì	to sign, to affix a signature
钱	qián	money, cash
前	qián	front; forward; in front of; preceding
前边	qiánbian	in front, ahead
前天	qiántiān	the day before yesterday
青	qīng	blue/green/black
请	qǐng	please; to invite
请问	qǐngwèn	may I ask…
去	qù	to go; away (after a verb, indicating action directed away from the speaker); past, previous
去年	qùnián	last year

R

人	rén	person, human
人民	rénmín	people

Characters	Pinyin	English
人民币	Rénmínbì	"People's currency," Chinese currency (RMB, ¥)
肉	ròu	meat
入	rù	to enter, to join

S

三	sān	three
三刻	sānkè	three-quarters of an hour, 45 minutes
商	shāng	business; a surname
商店	shāngdiàn	a shop, store
上	shàng	first, upper; to go up, to get on
上班	shàngbān	to go to work, to go to the office
上个	shàng ge	previous, first part of
上个星期	shàng ge xīngqī	last week
上个月	shàng ge yuè	last month
上课	shàngkè	to go to class, to teach a class
上午	shàngwǔ	morning
商学院	shāngxué-yuàn	business school

Characters	Pinyin	English
烧	shāo	to stew, to cook, to roast
勺子	sháozi	spoon
谁	shéi/shuí	Who?
生	shēng	to give birth to, to be born, to grow; life; raw
生日	shēngrì	birthday
什么	shénme	What?
十	shí	ten
时	shí	time, the present time, hour
是	shì	to be (am, is, are, was, were); yes, correct, right
室	shì	room; office
市	shì	market; city
是不是	shì búshì	Is it? Are they?
收	shōu	to accept, to receive
手	shǒu	hand
书	shū	book, document; to write
数	shǔ	to count
暑	shǔ	heat, hot weather
数	shù	number
双	shuāng	double, twin, pair

Characters	Pinyin	English
书店	shūdiàn	bookstore
谁	shuí/shéi	Who?
水	shuǐ	water
睡觉	shuìjiào	to go to bed, to sleep
睡午觉	shuì wǔjiào	to take a noon-time nap
丝	sī	threadlike, silk
四	sì	four
四月	sìyuè	April
送	sòng	to send, to deliver
素	sù	plain; vegetable
酸	suān	sour
酸辣汤	suānlàtāng	hot-and-sour soup
素菜	sùcài	vegetable dish
岁	suì	year of age, year old
所	suǒ	place; (measure word for buildings)
宿舍	sùshè	dorm

T

她	tā	she, her
台	tái	stand; (short form of 台湾 Taiwan)

Characters	Pinyin	English
太	tài	too, excessively, extremely
汤	tāng	soup
糖	táng	sugar, sweets, candy
糖醋	tángcù	sweet-and-sour (things)
天	tiān	day
条	tiáo	strip; measure word for long, narrow things
通	tōng	to lead to, to go through; open
头	tóu	head, chief, end
图	tú	picture, map
图书馆	túshūguǎn	library

W

外	wài	foreign country, the outside; external
外币	wàibì	foreign currency
外国	wàiguó	foreign country
外国人	wàiguórén	foreigner
外教	wàijiào	foreign teacher (short form of 外国教师 wàiguó jiàoshī)
外事处	wàishìchù	foreign affairs office

Characters	Pinyin	English
丸	wán	ball, pill, pellet
碗	wǎn	bowl
晚	wǎn	evening; late
晚饭	wǎnfàn	dinner
万	wàn	ten thousand
网	wǎng	net, Internet
网吧	wǎngbā	Internet cafe
往	wǎng/wàng	to go; toward, in the direction of
晚上	wǎnshang	evening, night
喂	wèi	hello
位	wèi	place; position
卫生纸	wèishēngzhǐ	toilet paper
文	wén	literature; writing
问	wèn	to ask
我	wǒ	I, me
我的	wǒde	my, mine
我们	wǒmen	we, us
五	wǔ	five
午	wǔ	noon
勿	wù	don't

Characters	*Pinyin*	*English*
午饭	wǔfàn	lunch

X

西	xī	west
息	xī	to rest
习	xí	to practice, to be used to; habit
洗	xǐ	to wash
系	xì	department (in a college)
虾	xiā	shrimp
下	xià	to go down, to get off; down, under, below; next
下班	xiàbān	to get out of work, to go off duty
下个	xià ge	next, second, latter
下个星期	xià ge xīngqī	next week
下个月	xià ge yuè	next month
下课	xiàkè	class is over, to dismiss class
先	xiān	first, before
现	xiàn	now, present
现在	xiànzài	now, present
香	xiāng	fragrant, appetizing

Characters	*Pinyin*	*English*
想	xiǎng	to want, to think
小	xiǎo	little, small, young
校	xiào	school
小姐	xiǎojie	Miss, Ms., young lady
下午	xiàwǔ	afternoon
些	xiē	some, a few; a little
谢谢	xièxie	thank you
新	xīn	new
星	xīng	star; a bit
行	xíng/háng	line, profession; to walk; OK
姓	xìng	to be surnamed; a surname, a family name
性	xìng	sex; nature; gender
星期	xīngqī	week
星期二	xīngqī'èr	Tuesday
星期几	xīngqījǐ	What day of the week?
星期六	xīngqīliù	Saturday
星期日	xīngqīrì	Sunday
星期三	xīngqīsān	Wednesday
星期四	xīngqīsì	Thursday
星期天	xīngqītiān	Sunday

Characters	Pinyin	English
星期五	xīngqīwǔ	Friday
星期一	xīngqīyī	Monday
修	xiū	to repair, to fix
休	xiū	to rest, to cease
休息	xiūxi	to rest
洗衣服	xǐ yīfu	to do laundry, to wash clothes
洗澡	xǐzǎo	to take a shower, to take a bath
需要	xūyào	to need
学	xué	to study, to learn; school, knowledge

Y

Characters	Pinyin	English
鸭	yā	duck
要	yào	to want, would like, need
也	yě	also
业	yè	profession; estate
一	yī	one
以	yǐ	at, on, of, with, by; to use
亿	yì	billion (hundred million)
一百	yìbǎi	one hundred
(一)点儿	(yì)diǎnr	a little; some

Characters	Pinyin	English
衣服	yīfu	clothes, clothing
一共	yígòng	altogether, in total
以后	yǐhòu	after; later on, afterwards; after
一会儿	yí huìr	in a moment, shortly, for a little while
衣架	yījià	hanger
一刻	yí kè	one quarter-hour, 15 minutes
姻	yīn	marriage; in-law
银	yín	silver, relating to money
饮	yǐn	a drink; to drink
英	yīng	Britain (short form of 英国 Yīngguó)
营	yíng	to operate, to run; to seek
英国人	Yīngguórén	British person
英文	Yīngwén	English language
英文系	yīngwénxì	English Department
英语	Yīngyǔ	English language
银行	yínháng	bank
饮料	yǐnliào	drinks, beverages
一起	yìqǐ	together
以前	yǐqián	prior to; ago; before

Characters	Pinyin	English
医院	yīyuàn	hospital
一直	yìzhí	straight, straight on, continuously
用	yòng	to use
由	yóu	reason; through
油	yóu	oil, grease
邮	yóu	post; to mail
有	yǒu	to have
右	yòu	right; right-hand
右边	yòubian	right side
邮局	yóujú	post office
有时候	yǒushíhòu	sometimes, at times
鱼	yú	fish
语	yǔ	language, words
元	yuán	¥1.00 (the basic unit of money), dollar
圆	yuán	¥1.00 (formal written form of 元 yuán), dollar
园	yuán	garden
远	yuǎn	far away, distant
月	yuè	month

Characters	Pinyin	English
Z		
在	zài	in, at; to be in, to be at, to exist
再	zài	again, still
再来	zài lái	come again, come back
早	zǎo	morning; early
早饭	zǎofàn	breakfast
早上	zǎoshang	morning
怎么	zěnme	How? In what way?
炸	zhá	to fry in oil, to deep fry
找	zhǎo	to look for, to seek; to give change
照	zhào	to photograph; license
这	zhè/zhèi	this
这边	zhèbian	this side, over here
这个	zhè ge/ zhèi ge	this one; this
这个星期	zhè ge xīngqī	this week
这个月	zhè ge yuè	this month
蒸	zhēng	to steam
正	zhēng/zhèng	first (in lunar calendar);

Characters	Pinyin	English
		upright; main
证	zhèng	certification, proof; to prove
这儿	zhèr	here
这些	zhèxiē	these
汁	zhī	juice
直	zhí	straight; vertical; frank
职	zhí	job, position
止	zhǐ	to prohibit, to stop
址	zhǐ	location, site
只有	zhǐyǒu	only; only if
中	zhōng	middle; China (short form of 中国 Zhōngguó)
钟	zhōng	clock, o'clock
中国	Zhōngguó	China
中国银行	Zhōngguó Yínháng	Bank of China
中间	zhōngjiān	middle, center; in between
钟头	zhōngtóu	hour
中文	Zhōngwén	Chinese language
中文系	zhōngwénxì	Chinese Department
中午	zhōngwǔ	noon

Characters	Pinyin	English
周	zhōu	week; cycle
周末	zhōumò	weekend
猪	zhū	pig
住	zhù	to live, to stay
转	zhuǎn/ zhuàn	to turn; to change; to rotate
猪肉	zhūròu	pork
子	zǐ	son; small; seed
自	zì	self; from
走	zǒu	to walk, to go, to leave
昨	zuó	yesterday, past
昨天	zuótiān	yesterday
左	zuǒ	the left; left-hand
左边	zuǒbian	left side
坐	zuò	to sit
做	zuò	to do; to be, to act as
作	zuò	to do, make; to act as; to write